BROADCAST YOUR VOICE

BROADCAST YOUR VOICE

Professional Secrets for Podcasting, Broadcasting, and Public Speaking

Michelle M. Mendoza

Find Your Voice Publishing

CONTENTS

CONTENTS

Dedication

I owe much thanks to the people who supported, believed in, and taught me in my passion for broadcasting. Mike Lennon "Justin Case", who started me on my radio journey, Kirby Wilbur who turned me on to talk radio, Dave Druy, my favorite "boss", and the many board ops, producers, co-workers, and fellow broadcasters who have been a part of my journey. Some were uplifting, others, well, I learned and grew from you. There are people like broadcaster and author Mark Griswold who helped me get my first book out and has been a spectacular friend. My buddies in broadcasting, Brent, Garrick, Del, Matt and those who are my favorite on air interview subjects, I thank you as well. To Josh, Giselle, and John who have always gone the extra mile for me, you are beyond amazing, and I forever appreciate you! To Carl who is my constant support and friend. I want to thank fans, listeners, viewers of my programs, you are the focus of sharing my voice. Finally, I give honor and glory to my Lord and Savior Jesus Christ, you are everything to me and I am grateful, so grateful for this broadcast journey that you called me to.

BROADCAST YOUR VOICE
Professional Secrets for Podcasting, Broadcasting, and Public Speaking

Copyright © 2023 by Michelle M. Mendoza

Published by

Find Your Voice Publishing

www.findyourvoice.fun

For questions or information regarding permission for excerpts or interviews please contact Find Your Voice Publishing and PR at contact@findyourvoice.fun

ISBN: 979-8-9883403-0-0 (paperback)
First Printing, 2023

CLEARING THE FOG

It was a ski adventure in the Cascade Mountain range. Standing trepidatiously at the top of a steep ridge, the weather suddenly changed. Fog and heavy snow descended, turning stunning vistas into a frosty veil. I was on a run that was too advanced for me, was unfamiliar with the terrain, and I was a bit scared. When visibility was reduced to just a few feet in front of me, my chest tightened, and my hands clenched my poles. I had no idea which way to go.

Luckily, I was accompanied by an expert level skier who knew the mountain well. I had a coach to encourage me in the right direction. He reminded me that the same fundamentals of the sport apply in any weather condition, with any visibility. His wisdom guided me through.

As we descended the mountain, we sank beneath the thick haze. Crisp blue skies opened to a stunning and much welcomed panorama. I finally knew exactly where I was going and how to get there. That sense of knowing is the relief that we all experience when the fog lifts and your direction is clear.

Some of the comments I hear most from those who are starting their communications effort, be it a broadcast, podcast, seminar, staged program, and the like, is that they need clarity on where to start, where to go, how to make things happen. There is so much to consider and so many directions. There is no reason to grope in the fog if you can be accompanied by an expert that can provide you with the direction that can make your efforts crystal clear.

The fog affects the novice as well as the professional. Our capability allows us to fly down the mountain with full confidence. Yet even the most capable can find that they've gone the wrong way or veered into unknown territory. They can discover that their equipment is not quite up to the task. To truly flourish the most successful people will rely on mentors, coaches, and will seek direction.

Houston Deck was the Park City, Utah-based athletic development coach for the U.S. Ski and Snowboard aerials and freeski teams that trained for the 2022 Winter Olympics in Beijing China. These next level athletes did not just go it alone when the stakes were high. They trained on and off the mountain. Houston was quoted in The Wall Street Journal as saying that even elite athletes start offseason training with basic fundamentals. "Whether it's an aerialist dropping from 50 feet in the air or an alpine athlete racing downhill at over 80 miles per hour, we like to say, 'Train the human, then the athlete. [1] '" Building on fundamentals from the soul up and training with someone in the know will help even professionals stay at the top of their game.

If you have ever skied, you have also fallen. You may recall trudging back up a hill in waist deep snow in search of equipment that flew in all directions after a tumble. You've had to pull yourself together with your feet, arms, body, poles, and skis facing every which way. Yet for the one who loves the feel of swishing through the quiet snow, taking in the unspoiled views, and experiencing the rush of being one with the mountain, there really isn't a bad day on the slopes.

The same can be said for expressing your passion, your voice. Mistakes, misspoken words, and failed equipment are no more fun than tumbling down a mountain. However, the fulfillment you receive from the pursuit of your purpose outweighs any small flicker of failure and makes you better at your craft in the process.

There is something even deeper than the glory of doing what you were meant to do. When you share your voice, you are giving a part of your soul to your audience, a piece of your experience and knowledge. You are making a difference in someone else's life and there are few things in life that feel as good as giving.

It has been said that it is truly better to give than to receive. Science has weighed this out. There has been countless research showing how pleasure centers of the brain ignite when people choose to do something beneficial, selfless, or kind for others. Whatever your calling, your purpose will be more fulfilling when you move the emphasis from to others. This is your first step towards true clarity.

My older sister was 25, so young, too young to suffer through breast cancer. She and her husband Greg were an integral part of my tween and teen years. They took me to auto races, seaside vacations, horseback riding adventures, and together we learned to ski. Marcia had a lust for life but as the cancer crept through her body and the chemotherapy zapped her strength, my visits with her went from exciting exploits to weekends hanging out in her bedroom.

Teenagers can feel like life will go on forever, death seemed elusive. I was just 15 years old, but the reality of life's finite nature started to unveil. I passed out cold when I first saw the massive needle and strange glowing serum of chemicals that doctors would shoot into her veins. I felt an emptiness in the pit of my stomach as I watched her pull out her beautiful thick dark hair by the handfuls. I hurt along with her when I saw the sadness in her eyes as she tried to draw on eyebrows and normalize fake eyelashes.

One weekend I stayed with her when her husband was away for work. She rested throughout the afternoon in hopes of having enough energy to take me to her favorite Italian restaurant the next day. That night, while she slept, I stayed up. I spent the entire night customizing her fake eyelashes. Hair by hair I split, clipped, and combed painstakingly to match my own. Marcia wore those eyelashes beautifully until her death months later.

I was spoiled, sometimes selfish, I cared mostly for my own interests at that point in my life. Even growing up in church with verses reminding me to, "esteem others greater than ourselves," and "It is better to give than to receive," I was still more self-focused than focused on others. That one act of selfless love for my sister awakened a limitless joy that even the sadness of her illness could not quell. The reward of her appreciation was priceless. The lesson of using my efforts to benefit others came alive that day.

When starting any venture or looking to grow and improve on a journey that you have already started, there will be moments of frustration and confusion. Things will go right, and things will suddenly go wrong. Everyone needs help and direction. Developing fundamentals will prepare you. Having assistance to lead you through the fog will get you moving. Learning your craft, the needed equipment, and how to build your efforts will clear the fog. But turning your passion into a purpose that serves others will make crystal clear how to move forward and will bring joy as you share your voice.

[1] Murphy, J. (2020) "The Workout Olympic Skiers Use to Prepare for the Slopes," The Wall Street Journal , 19 December. Available at: https://www.wsj.com/articles/the-workout-olympic-skiers-use-to-prepare-for-the-slopes-11608375600 (Accessed: February 19, 2023).

SETTING THE STAGE

He carved out a spectacular career from humble beginnings. Tim Tebow is a two-time national champion, Heisman Trophy winner, first-round NFL draft pick, and a former professional baseball player. Tim has become an athletic icon. He is also an author, having four New York Times best-selling books. He is an effective communicator, as an international speaker, and football analyst. He is an actor and executive producer. In addition to all of this, Tim is a man of faith and philanthropy as well.

Tim Tebow's fame and accomplishments are striking, considering his homeschooled beginnings as a son to Philippine missionaries. He wasn't even supposed to live. Pamela, Tim's mother contracted amoebic dysentery and fell into a coma while pregnant with him. Doctors recommended aborting him, but his parents refused and gave birth to a child that grew up to impact American society.

Tim's story can be an encouragement to anyone with a passion. Where you come from, what obstacles you face, being cut from the team, having to reinvent yourself, suffering ridicule, need not stop you from powering on and achieving your dreams. Be unstoppable.

Each of the outlets of Tim's life has been acted out on differing platforms. Each platform is where he has stood for a time to showcase his passion. The platforms were of player, commentator, writer, actor, son, and later, husband. We too may have many platforms resulting from the many interests of our life. Each one is enhanced by our past experiences, lessons learned, personal growth, and natural talents. They are also affected by our communication superpowers.

There are four communication superpowers. They are the elements that every communication effort needs to truly succeed. These super-powers of entertainer, engager, informer, or inspirer will help to push us to excellence. We naturally go where our talents, gifting, and super-powers flow. Our performance is then heightened as we acquire and develop the powers that we are less gifted in.

Some of the roles we master as though our superpower was custom made for it. Other roles we may think we are perfect for we fall flat in. Why? It is because talent alone will not guarantee success, we must have the right focus, training, and platform that fits our passion and gifting. Choosing the right stage for your voice is paramount.

Frank Nappi's critically acclaimed novel, "The Legend of Mickey Tus-sler", was produced into the made-for-television sports drama, "A Mile in His Shoes", in 2011. It tells the story of an autistic boy, Mickey, who was confined to his family's farm by his protective father. When a minor league manager happened upon their property, he discovered Mickey throwing apples the size of baseballs into a metal tub for his pigs. The balls flew at lightning speed with professional accuracy.

The manager set out to convince his father that his son's talent is unique, that he is gifted, and that he could have a future they had never imagined. He challenged them to see Mickey through his talent and passion instead of through the fear of failure, disappointment, or disability.

The movie's inspirational message shows what is possible when faith, integrity, and perseverance empower us. With the right coaching and direction anyone can develop their talent and when directed onto the right platform, it will shine. The unlikely can become a reality.

In the film, Mickey has a near breakdown, caused by frustration when trying to learn something new. It was a pitch called the knuckle ball. The knuckle ball, the coach said, is unpredictable. It is nearly impossible to hit because not even the ball knows where it will go.

Your communication effort will sometimes be like Mickey's knuckle ball. No one knows what will happen in the future, the ball does not know where it will go. However, with the right foundation, the proper stage, and fantastic aim, you can know that things will go in the right direction. You can build a platform for success.

Broadcast Your Voice picks up where the book Find Your Voice leaves off. We are building on the passion, talent, and background that makes up and empowers your voice. We are employing the superpowers to level up your message. We are sifting through endless platforms to find the right fit for your voice. Whether broadcasting, podcasting, teaching, public speaking, or interpersonal communication, evaluate before you jump down the mountain. Examine the many outlets and choose well the platform you will play upon. This is the foundation that, when laid, will help make the rest of your message fall easily into place. It will get you through the fog.

3

COMMUNICATION FOUNDATION

Karen's dad treated us to double scoop ice cream cones for washing his car on a warm early October day. Displayed before us were dozens of delicious flavor options to choose from. With Halloween right around the corner, we made an unfortunate choice of color over content. The stark bright orange sherbet and deep black liquorish ice cream looked amazing. Digging my tongue into the center between the flavors, I soon realized that I had made a terrible gastronomic mistake. That was the all-time nastiest flavor combination I may have experienced in my life. Decades later, it still makes me shiver in disgust. Communication outlets, like ice cream flavors, come in many forms. Choosing the right combination is paramount.

Like ice cream in a freezer case, there are many broadcast options to consider. Broadcasting encompasses a myriad of markets on television, radio, internet, and any mass communication medium, stage, and screen. You can utilize a talk format, a news format, entertainment format, among others. Live and in person communications can be lectures, whiteboard lessons, or a monologue. Podcasting is the broadcast of spoken words over the internet and vodcasting is video podcasting. There are interview formats, color commentaries, call-in discussions, or questions and answer formats. In choosing a platform, you are choosing the best flavor for your efforts and a vehicle to transmit your message to your audience.

IKEA, the Swedish-founded ready-to-assemble furniture company, had a commercial once that showed the importance of choosing the right vehicle. It touted a tiny compact car trudging precariously down the road with boxes upon boxes of their products tethered to the roof, tripling the car's height. The boxes wobbled along atop the bright yellow car until it came to a low-hanging bridge. If you are taking a trip to IKEA, you might choose a more adequate vehicle than a tiny yellow compact car.

Likewise, what you choose as your platform for messaging is the vehicle that presents your voice to your audience. Choose wisely. Like choosing a sports car, a work truck, a jeep, or fuel saver for getting where you need to go, your broadcast choice should be determined by the job you want done, the audience you're reaching out to, and the presentation style that is right for your message.

Narrow down your choices. The more focused you are the more successful you will be. Liken it to transportation vehicles which have three basic types, land, sea, or air. Narrowing that down further, you have work, pleasure, or personal vehicles. Then you will decide if it must be large or small, powerful, or economical, luxurious, or cost effective.

Communication efforts are much the same. Choosing the precise vehicle or platform for your message is easiest if you understand your needs. Who are you, what are you trying to accomplish, and to whom are you reaching out. Decisiveness makes a world of difference in the planning of your program and platform.

As there are three basic types of transportation vehicles, there are three basic types of broadcast focuses. They are topical , ideological, and experiential . One of these will be the ground floor of your efforts.

THREE BROADCAST FOCUSES
TOPICAL OR INFORMATION BASED COMMUNICATIONS
Information based broadcasts or communications can also be referred to as topic based. This type of broadcast is for communicators that are highly focused on an issue or topic. If you wish to educate an audience

about antique autos, climate science, the benefits of group sports for children, or women's health, this format is for you.

IDEOLOGICAL BASED COMMUNICATIONS

An ideological or idea-based broadcast or communication effort focuses on a belief, perspective, or idea that is held in high regard to yourself and to your audience. You and your target market may be strong believers in animal rights, or you may have a faith-based philosophy. You might wish to cover health and your passion lies in naturopathic remedies and treatments that align with the idea that the body has a beautiful ability to self-heal. This category is also for those who may have a strong drive or belief in a political ideology.

Ideological based communications show enthusiasm for or loyalty to a segment of the population or group who is like minded. Liken it to groups that you might find on social media. Those groups' titles and categories can be the basis for ideologically based broadcasts when the group is assembled due to a common belief.

EXPERIENTIAL BASED COMMUNICATIONS

Experience based broadcasts or communications gather a following of people with a shared background or reality. Like ideological based broadcasts, the experience-based audiences are a group, but they do not necessarily have a shared belief. Rather, they are united because they share something similar in the happenstance of life.

A mom's group that shares antidotes and craft ideas for toddlers, homeschooling parents, men over the age of 50, survivors of cancer, these are experience based groups. The members may differ in politics, religion, and other fundamental ideological leanings but they are brought together because they have a shared life experience.

The comb of the honeybee is an example of both the marvel of nature and the importance of a good foundation. The hive's comb is shelter, nursery, and pantry for the bees. With diligence, every little creature in the hive works purposefully, building, filling, and cleaning the hexagonal cells of their hive home.

In feral hives, bees create comb in differing sizes and speed depending on their needs. They clean it out regularly for a hygienic environment. In nature, when the cells have outlived their usefulness, absorb toxins, or become unhealthy, the bees cut a portion of the comb out and replace it with fresh, pristine, virgin comb. They push it to the bottom of the hive where workers bees fly it out like little environmental hazmat laborers.

Commercial apiary practices changed that by forcing the bees to create comb on a pre-set plastic hive foundation, created in the largest cell size possible for maximum honey production. The pre-formed plastic comb is seldom replaced, which forces bees to use and re-use the same comb again and again. The larger size foundation also makes larger brood cells, of unhatched baby bees, seal in gestation longer than in nature. This subjects them to brood diseases that are much less likely in wild settings.

Is there a road back for bees who have been subjected to man's interference? Many beekeepers are abandoning the standard, man-made practices for more natural bee keeping policies. When they do, hives can quickly bounce back as bees remember their D.N.A. training. The bees revert to healthy practices that serve their hive best.

Check your communication foundation. You may be trudging along, like the bees, but your foundation may not be providing the best base for your efforts. Luckily, you can bounce back by relying on good training, and rebuilding on a better base.

4

BUILD YOUR PLATFORM

Kurtis was a talented actor, having spent time on Broadway alongside some of the greats. He could sing, dance, and had a firm acting foundation that highlighted his exceptional gifting. In between gigs he took work filming an industrial movie for the military with me as his co-star.

The 10-day schedule left down time for cast and crew to infiltrate the small city where filming was taking place. Each evening they would gather for meals and entertainment. One night at karaoke, the importance of choosing the right platform and audience became apparent.

Kurtis took the stage, and with a voice that could make angels take notice, he belted out a song worthy of raucous applause. Instead, you could hear crickets in the room with the local's lackluster response when he finished his performance. I followed him, singing a Tanya Tucker song and the crowd nearly ate themselves alive in appreciation. Come to find out we were at a women's only establishment. It was the kind of place that men were just not welcomed, and Kurtis' talent was not appreciated.

Choosing the wrong outlet and structure for your voice will keep you from reaching the right audience. Your faithful followers will know what you're about as your platform provides consistency. There's nothing wrong with a few surprises and tweaks but your continued efforts are like a contract of reliability with your audience. Continuity builds audiences.

The base you choose for your communication effort is foundational. Like building a home, you pour your foundation then build upon it. Establish your stage on the topical, ideological, or experiential foundation. Next, choose a communication platform that can start to shape what your topical, ideological, or experience-based broadcast will look like?

According to a senior lecturer and head of the Department of Mass Communication at Alex Ekwueme Federal University, Ngozi Eje Uduma, "broadcasts will all fall under one of the broadcast categories of entertainment , education , talk , news, or children's programs [1] . " This is the next level of your message formation. Which of these fits your vision?

Step by step, the blueprint of your passion should come together. Your message finds its foundation of topical, ideological, or experiential communication. You build on it your platform of entertainment, education, talk, news, or children's programing. Now you can start to flesh out the particulars that make the structure of your communication effort uniquely yours.

Many renown theaters around the world showcase a particular specialty. The National Noh Theatre in Tokyo, Japan is constructed from 400-year-old cypress trees. Its name, 'Noh', means 'skill' or 'talent'. The theater is known for spectacular presentations of traditional Japanese musical dramas and plays. Shakespeare's Globe theater is an iconic structure rebuilt to near exact specifications of its 1613 glory after a fire destroyed the original structure. This historic theater can be counted on to produce Shakespearian productions. The Palais Garnier is in Paris, France. Its six-ton chandelier once plummeted from the ceiling in 1896 killing an audience member. The incident inspired a famous scene in Gaston Leroux's novel, " The Phantom of the Opera." It is still known for grand staircases and an exquisite stage that presents operas and ballets.

Performances on the stages of these theaters boast a reliably consistent product. Those standing on their platforms present distinct crafts or a type of performance. What do you want to be known for? What is your niche? Your platform must find its own specialty.

[1] Duyile, A. (2005). Broadcast News Reporting and Programming. Akure: Endurance Prints & Publishers

5

FORMATS OF COMMUNICATION

The car was on its side filling quickly with water. I stood on the seat banging and tugging at the shorted out automatic window hoping to escape. Climbing from the seat to the head rest, I had only a foot left of air. Finality crossed my mind.

It was a stormy Christmas eve; the road was entirely hidden under a dark watery layer. It was impossible to gauge how deep it truly was. This road shaved twenty minutes off my route. So, when I saw a little car driving out on the other side of this huge pool, I decided that if they could make it so could I. What I didn't realize is that the little car did not drive through the water, they had chosen to turn around to avoid disaster. Ten yards in, my car was whisked away and I with it.

The next day my car was on the front page of the local newspaper. The headline read, "This driver lucky to escape as winter storm wreaks havoc." I had managed to shimmy the window open, crawl out, and stand on the car's rooftop to await help. A hero in a massive four-wheel-drive braved the storm and brought me to safety. Having lived and learned, I am now quite reluctant to rush into standing water without weighing the situation and looking at alternative routes.

Recalling that experience reminds me of the paths we choose in life. What seems the most expedient route can also hold unanticipated difficulties. As you flesh out your communication efforts, there are so many routes you can take. Your presentation can follow one of many formats or become a compilation of any combination. Knowing the concerns before you choose a route may save you from forging ahead without care.

Below, you will find the main formats of communication. They each have a glorious draw and their own drawbacks. Examine each and decide which would best fit your voice.

FORMATS - THE PLATFORMS FOR COMMUNICATION
LECTURE PRESENTATIONS

A Lecture presentation is what you experience with a TED TALK. TED Talks showcase speakers and ideas in talks that are under 20 minutes. T.E.D is an acronym for technology, entertainment, and design. Lectures, speeches, or talks of any kind can grant your audience insight into the topic of your passion. They can give you unique perspective, present new and fascinating discoveries, highlight knowledge or expertise, or demonstrate innovations.

Pros:

This format can highlight your focused interest and expertise. You control most of the variables.

Cons:

There is a reason that TED talks are under 20 minutes in length. This format can get dry and boring very quickly.

PERFORMANCE PRESENTATIONS

This type of presentation gives your audience performance after performance. Whether music, comedy, dance, or poetry, it is a showcase of talent. Performance presentations might include some banter, introductions, short interviews, or commentary, but they are primarily presentations of performance in nature.

Pros:

This format is a wonderful way to showcase talent. As a picture, specifically a moving one, is worth 1,000 words, a performance can say much with the expression of talen.

Cons:

A performance alone can leave your audience wanting more of a connection with the performer. We have been conditioned to expect a kind of relationship with the broadcaster that performance alone cannot give.

SCRIPTED PRESENTATIONS

Most broadcasters utilize some sort of script. Few are completely ad-libbed. A scripted presentation is not simply the guidelines a presenter follows. A scripted presentation is an episodic or dramatic series. Like taking a chapter or portion from your favorite book. It can be presented in a radio drama or a live dramatic read format. The broadcast may be fictitious or based on a real story. It will still focus on telling its tale to a focused group based on a common interest in information, an ideology, or shared experience.

Pros:

This format is entertaining, and can be informative, engaging, and inspiring as well.

Cons :

This is one of the hardest and most labor-intensive formats to produce. Unless you are doing a simple 'book reading', bringing all the elements of sound, sight, and story together can burn you out quickly. Additionally, if you are telling a true story, it is vital to get all your facts straight, lest you lose respect with your audience.

INTERVIEWS

The beauty of the interview presentation is that, as the broadcaster, you do not have to be an expert in any given area. You can simply employ the expertise of others in a chosen field. Interviews can be question and answer or conversational in nature. Interviews bring the knowledge and experience of your guest to your audience and vice versa when you are being interviewed.

If you are on the other side of the microphone, an interview will give you the stage for highlighting your passion. It can be a free way to present the world with your pitch, idea, book, or product. Interviews can be an engaging experience.

Pros:

Again, interviews are a spectacular way of expanding our own expertise by utilizing someone else's. Interviews bring your audience into a conversation that they otherwise might never have with someone they might never meet. They can additionally be a commercial for your message when being interviewed.

Cons:

There is an art to interviewing and being interviewed that many do not understand. As highlighted in this book, many a star has tried to do interview style talk shows and failed. Learning to ask the right questions, keeping a good pace, being able to gracefully stop an interviewee from droning on, keeping control of the conversation without seeming ridged, takes skill, talent, and practice.

Additionally, as the interviewee, having compelling stories to share, learning to talk in sound bites, and presenting an interesting interview is vital.

CONVERSATION/DIALOGUE

Conversation presentations bring the host and a partner, guest host, or guest into dialogue on a given subject. It is as though you toss out a story, news item, subject, or thought on the table and the participants dive in. They share their thoughts, opinions, antidotes, researched facts, and ideas.

Pros:

This is one of the most entertaining and lively forms of broadcast. From the 'View,' to round table sports talk shows, the banter can be a joy for the audience. You also relieve the host from carrying the entire weight of the show. They do not have to be the only one being clever, interesting, or informative to draw in followers.

Cons:

The conversation model can sometimes exclude the audience and leave them feeling on the outside of a party looking in. The participants can be so caught up in their own engagement that they fail to engage with the audience.

MONOLOGUE

In the acting world a monologue is a long speech or segment presented by just one actor in a play or production. A monologue in the broadcaster's world is a solo performance of information streaming from one person. The host opines on an idea or issue. He may also have a written or scripted piece that is read to the audience. A monologue is usually centered on a single ideology or point.

Pros:

A monologue is an efficient way to present an important idea, manifesto, or statement. There is no one to interrupt the flow as the presenter controls the broadcast.

Cons:

A monologue is usually read, recited, or ad-libbed. This can get dull in short order without passion, inspiration, or an entertainment factor.

NEWS

Just like tuning in to the evening news, a news broadcast takes news stories and reports them. Commentary is common and can add connection and interest to your audience, but a news format focuses almost solely on the sharing of unadulterated news.

Some news formats will color the story, spin the wording, highlight certain portions. It is an attempt to manipulate the audience or feed their fears and tickling ears. This is not real news. It does fall under the format of news style broadcasts and can appear to be news, but it is more in line with propaganda. True news is the non-biased reporting of actual confirmed stories.

Pros:

This is a very easy way to break into broadcasting. There is no end to stories, and your content comes pre-scripted from a professional writer. Make certain that you attribute any news that you utilize.

Cons:

News can be dry. Professional broadcast studios fall into the trap of 'if it bleeds it leads' to boost audience ratings. It is easy to allow sensationalism to take control. News in our era is not always well researched or confirmed. Report a non-confirmed false story and you may lose credibility with your audience.

COMMENTARY

Commentary communication is the editorializing of news and information. It is often used in conjunction with news programming. Reporters may be referred to as an analyst, pundit, summarizer. The commentary presentation is the 'Monday morning quarterbacking' of the broadcast experience. Usually found in the sports realm, a 'colorcaster' will give commentary beyond just the factual play by play of an event.

A famous non-sports example is an American television series called 'Mystery Science Theater 3000'. This comedic sci-fi show has a janitor and his two sentient robot companions trapped like animals in a zoo under observation by mad scientists called 'mads'. The 'mads' force them to watch and comment on B rated films. Their 'riffing' is a color commentary that takes some of the worst films in human history and turns them into a hilarious experience.

A broadcast of color commentary can talk about a story, news items, people, events. It can view an entire event or provide analysis from clips of an event. Commentary is your opinion set in motion.

Pros:

Color commentary can be fun, lively, entertaining, maddening, engaging. You can learn from it or be enraged by it if you disagree. These elements make for a good broadcast.

Cons:

It can be hard to know when to turn off the comments. Many a commentator has found themselves going too far as they ad-lib ideas. Commentary without reins can run amok and become untrustworthy when not accompanied by solid facts.

CALL-IN FORMAT

In a call-in presentation your audience becomes the guests of the program. Like a conversation format, presentation of topics, ideas, news stories, or issues are laid out by the presenter who then invites willing participants to either phone in, text, email, comment below, or step up to the mic. The audience member may ask questions, give thoughts and remarks in interaction with the host.

Pros:

There is no better way to build audience loyalty and engagement than directly speaking with them. It is well known in talk radio that for every caller who takes the time to phone in, there are many, many others who share their thoughts and do not connect. An audience member can find it easy to relate to other audience members.

Cons:

Building your audience to the point of having a steady stream of reliable callers takes time. Having a phone screener when they do phone in can help 'screen out' callers that will not contribute well to your efforts. Not everyone who calls in will be audible and sometimes mentally able to engage. Taking calls requires the art of helping others to find and express their voice. It requires intuition in knowing when to cut someone off and out. This can take time to develop.

Q & A PRESENTATIONS

Like call-in presentations, Q & A, or question and answer formats invite the ponderings of the audience and those like them. The host may use 'listener mail' or take on common questions pertaining to a given subject. The questions can be answered by the host, a guest, or other participants. There can be elements of expertise or apologetics to this format.

Pros:

Everyone has questions and everyone is looking for the answers. A Q & A show gives them what they are looking for, satiating a need in this information age. The internet can sometimes provide answers, but it is impersonal, and people often wonder who to trust. Your audience trusts you and the answers you provide.

Cons:

Fake news. That word is batted around like a ball in a volleyball match. The idea of not knowing whom you can trust is a real concern. When answering questions, the host puts themselves in the seat of a perceived expert. With great power comes great responsibility and the opportunity to get it wrong and subsequently lose your audience. You must also be prepared to get an onslaught of angry people who disagree.

CHALKBOARD FORMAT

Chalkboard presentations refer to a lesson or fact illustrated in creative ways. It is usually formatted for video where you might see a white board drawing of nothing more than a hand and pen quickly scribbling out pictures that illustrate a narration. It may be a cartoon or series of pictures that do the same. Sometimes there is narration. Sometimes there is nothing more than words across a screen with music. There are apps and sites that can quickly produce a chalkboard presentation with just a little input. A.I. is developing quickly in this field. The audio equivalent is narration with music and sound effects that enhance the presentation.

Pros:

This format is a marvelous teaching tool. It can hit many of the learning styles of visual, auditory, and reading. Chalkboard presentations, like PowerPoint presentations, catch your audience's eye and make your message memorable.

Cons:

Production is a lot of work. While there are programs that can help create presentations, it can take much time and effort. If all your presentations are sound and pictures only you may lose engagement unless you add a speaker.

DEMONSTRATIVE

An ideal outlet for the tactile tinkerer or an expert who wants to share their craft is demonstrative productions. It is where you show your audience how to do something you know well. From how to fix a carburetor, to how to navigate a computer program, it is an outlet for the DIY 'wanna be'. These broadcasts walk a person through a process, showing them how to get from point A to point B.

Pros:

DIY is one of the most googled elements in every subject; the market is huge.

Cons:

It is important to know what you are doing. Never waste your audience's time or they will never return. Making sure you are clear and concise is key.

MAGAZINE OR VARIETY STYLE

A magazine or variety presentation takes many aspects of presentations and unites them under one heavily promoted theme. Let's cite a fictitious podcast, Jenny Joy's The Joy of Motherhood Podcast. Jenny takes on many ideas and topics in each episode. She may simply present a few funny stories about the crazy things that kids say and do. The next episode, she may take calls to allow the audience to tell their tales. Other days she might have a funny chalkboard presentation about teaching her son to tie his shoes, rattle off a monologue about date night with her husband, or give color commentary on a P.T.A. decision. Yet, Jinny brings consistency by tying every episode securely to her theme, audience, and purpose.

Pros:

This format utilizes the best of all the styles.

Cons:

This format also assumes the challenges of all the styles.

Every journey you make in life and in communication has its pros and cons. Some routes we choose for expedience and others for enjoyment. Your communication efforts should always be a mixture of both.

6

PICK YOUR PEOPLE

Let me introduce you to a fictional podcaster. Joe Giggly. Joe is an amateur comedian. He's the guy who can find humor anywhere. Joe can add a quick-witted quip to any conversation; he keeps his friends and family in stiches. Joe is also a husband, father, and hard-working provider. When he can fit it in between work, house duties, and coaching little league for his son Buck, Joe will take a night off and do standup at the local comedy club.

Joe's once passionate vision of finding himself on the big stage or getting a bit on a late-night talk show started to dwindle. The cares of life and responsibilities of being a husband and a father replaced the dreams of his youth. But growing older does not mean that one's purpose and passion cannot find fulfillment. Joe merged his reality with his dreams and started a humor-ridden podcast called Legacy Laughter.

Joe is focused on an audience that he understands well. His niched target is fathers who need connection. Life gets busy and before they know it, their dreams have passed them by. Joe brings these dreaming dads together with anecdotes, comedy, laughter, and hope.

Let's view the blueprints of Joe's efforts for an example of how a communication effort is built. We start with the foundation. Joe's podcast would be a shared experience broadcast. Joe's platform is a talk format. Joe does interviews and will sometimes field calls from his audience. If he presented only stand-up comedy and a few introductions he would fall under the entertainment category. Joe might have chosen to report on funny news stories that pertain to fathers, then he would be in the news category. Joe can still have educational, entertaining, or newsy elements but he is primarily an experience-based variety-talk format program.

Can you see how the specific format approach can offer you a sense of what your outlet will be and what your efforts will look like? I have listened to hundreds of podcasts that lack a sense of direction, understanding of who they are, what they're trying to do, and who they are trying to do it for. Every person that I have consulted has asked for help in finding clarity. With a formatted construction, a whole new level of success is possible.

Before Joe goes to air, he must hyper focus on the most important aspect of his efforts. It is the who. He must pick his people. He must have a pinpoint focus on who he is trying to help. The more exact he is in creating an ideal audience, the more successful he will be at reaching them. You cannot find a specific address if all you know is a general location.

You, like our fictional example of Joe Giggly, have life experiences, knowledge, communications strengths, and weaknesses. Read the book Find Your Voice: Your Superpower and Passion Unleashed to learn more about using your unique make up to empower your voice. Discover what superpowers are needed to succeed. Your unique nuances are perfect for reaching an ideal niche of people.

Before you get on stage, turn on the mic, and begin speaking, create in your mind the avatar of your ideal audience. Who are they, what do they believe? Where do they live, work, play? How do they spend their free time, their money? What do they look like, drive, do for fun? Most importantly, how can you solve a problem or dilemma for them? How can you make a difference in their lives?

Your audience will be drawn to you when they know you have something they need. If you solve a problem or answer a question that they are already asking, you are meeting a need. You become valuable to their lives.

Joe Giggly knows the feeling of disconnection and lost dreams. He understands the struggle of men in their quest to be good husbands, fathers, providers, and yet also want to feel vital and hopeful. He is reaching men in middle America with young children. They are married, in their late 30s, own their first home, and drive a vehicle that is suitable for the family when they wish they had a sports car. They are men who just want to connect with likeminded men for an hour or so a week. They want to laugh, relate, and walk away encouraged, ready to be a better man.

For your efforts, wherever you communicate and whatever it is that your message holds, you are speaking to the air if you do not have an audience. You can be an orator with the voice of an angel. You can have knowledge that can change the world. If you do not pick your people and find your niched audience, your effort will always fall short.

7 |

WHEN AND WHERE

Once your foundation is laid, your platform takes on form, and you know to whom you will target your message, it is as though your efforts becoming a structure. Your building is ready for paint, window coverings, and furnishings.

It is time to fill in the fine details like when you will communicate, broadcast, speak, share. Where will you communicate from and to? What equipment will you require? How often will you broadcast?

You may choose to do one presentation and give it again and again in many locations. You may have a one and done program. You might broadcast monthly, bi-weekly or one or more times per week. Will your production be 5 minutes, 10-15, 15-30, 30 to 45, or over an hour? Once your production blueprint has been drawn out, your structure is formed, then this last bit of detail is like decorating the rooms.

Between 2000 and 2008 a program called Trading Spaces aired on American television. It was a kind of do-it-yourself design show. On the program, a set of neighbors would re-decorate a room in each other's home with the help of a professional designer. They had a limited amount of time and budget, and the homeowner had no say in how the room would turn out.

Viewers could relate to the anxiety of homeowners who stood, eyes closed, waiting for the reveal of a room that they had no say in what would happen to it. They could feel the homeowners joy in a beautiful

| 27 |

result. They would cringe when the room turned out to be a design disaster.

One of the worst failures in Trading Spaces history was "the beach room". The project ended with what looked like cheap plastic material of bold yellow and red stripes covering the walls and ceiling of this living room. The walls were meant to resemble a beach umbrella but left the room looking more like a sad circus tent. The only furniture in the room was two beach chairs and a hideous fake tree with clashing material made into fronds. The floor of this interior room was the worst part. The designer had the participants haul in load after load of sand. The sand covered the floor wall-to-wall, making a horrifying mess. The result was garish and arguably the worst of the shows' outcomes.

Here is a professional secret that will help you succeed in your efforts, read the room. These designers were driven by their own creative desires and ideas but failed to focus on the client and their needs. A healthy mix of both will create a beautiful outcome. You will have successful direction at every level, including when, where, and how often to broadcast, when you blend your desires with a focus on your audience. What would your idyllic follower want and need and what can you provide?

Consider this in relation to your schedule and when to broadcast. Beyond what works for you, think of what your audience would want. What day, time, hour, would benefit them?

As for length, if you are giving a one-time talk, your presentation should be long enough to satisfy the audience's needs. Make their investment of time worthwhile but not so long that they get bored. Attention span is always a factor and less is often more as far as length is concerned. Attention is assured only if the seat can endure. Find balance between giving good information and not overwhelming or dragging on.

As for frequency. For repeated efforts, connect with your audience frequently enough that you will not be forgotten. Broadcast so that you can build on previous episodes. Make certain that you have fresh and engaging content to fill the time.

Next is how. How will your efforts be presented. In broadcasting, you have commercial broadcasting, public broadcasting, and community broadcasting. Commercial broadcasting is for profit. Public broadcasting is not for profit and is supported by donations, grants, and to a lesser extent, subscriptions. Community broadcasts are focused on providing service to an established community. Community broadcasts can be either for or not for profit.

How ever your platform takes its shape, and whatever you dress it up with, remember that consistency is an agreement made between you and your audience. It is a contract that says, "This is what you will get when you tune in." Your ideal follower likes what you do and knows what to expect. Thus, they will return for more.

Imagine your favorite restaurant. This restaurant holds a special place in your culinary mind. You return to it because you know what they will be serving. They may have off-menu specials now and then, but you still know what to expect when you go there. Combining morsels of other elements to your broadcast can add interest, it is the broadcast equivalent of a restaurant's special of the day. Never forget, however, what your bread and butter is. That stability breeds sustainability.

If for some reason you build a format and it ends up looking like a bad episode of a design show, do not be afraid to revisit your structure, tweak things, add elements, and change it up. The famous basketball star Michael Jordan may be quite successful, yet he is quoted as saying, "I've missed more than 9000 shots in my career. I've lost almost 300 games. 26 times, I've been trusted to take the game winning shot and missed. I've failed over and over and over again in my life. And that is why I succeed." [1] It is not the gifted, the talented, or even the lucky that truly succeed, it is the persistent.

[1] Michael Jordan – 'FAILURE COMMERCIAL' Nike Corporation, 2019.

8

GETTING EQUIPPED

May 2017. It was just before they hit the ice in Roger's Place Stadium to play game three of the Western Conference Second Round of the National Hockey League playoffs. In Edmonton, an Alberta based country music singer Brett Kissel did the honors of singing both the Canadian and U.S. national anthems. That is, until a mic malfunction dropped his voice part way through the Star-Spangled Banner. You will never find an Oiler's fan cheering for the Anaheim Ducks in a home match-up. We did, however, hear 18,000 Oiler fans sing the other country's anthem when the mic went silent. That sportsmanship was something to behold. Acapella voices gave respect to a sister nation and their rivals before a match.

If there is a way that equipment can malfunction during a live broadcast, I can pretty much assure you that I have experienced it! Additionally, I've experienced it live on air in front of tens of thousands of listeners or viewers. When you communicate from your genuine self to your ideal listener it is easy to take on all disasters with genuine sincerity and make opportunities out of calamity.

On one live radio broadcast in a major market, the power went out just as I got on air. The backup generator kept me live but the computers, phone lines, and all other systems were out. Everything that I had planned for my 3-hour show was useless. No guests. No listener calls. No internet for news stories. Even my notes were on the computer that sat lifeless before me.

The show must go on. I spent the first half of the show telling life stories from the heart, my testimony if you will. When the power came on in the second half of the show and all systems were go, the phone lines exploded with listeners that were moved and engaged. The best way to handle those mayhem moments is by taking charge and being the real you.

Mayhem is what can separate the novice in you from the professional you are continuously becoming. Those situations will have you walking out the other side with real-world training on how to handle anything that comes your way. If you can handle on-air disasters, everyday broadcasting is a sunny walk in the park.

Having said that, trust me, I would prefer working equipment to real world lessons any day of the week! If all the world is a stage, I don't just need better lighting. I need a working sound system, ample amplification, reliable computer applications, and could you, please, toss in a professional engineer?

Whatever your chosen mode for sharing your voice, somewhere along the line you will need equipment. You may find that you will want to record. You might desire to share that recording to email, post a podcast, attach it to your website, create a video platform, or make a social media post. Whether just starting your communication's journey or if you have a broadcast studio at hand, examining your equipment in light of your purpose is always a good idea and can keep you from those mayhem moments.

My surrogate grandpa had a woodshop in the garage behind our home with just about any woodworking tool known to man. I'd sit on the workbench after school and watch him tinker. He used to say, "Whatever the job, pick the right tools".

If your efforts are to podcast or to post on social media, have the right tools. If you are standing up on stage, pick the right tools. If your efforts are to make money, to start a business, to indulge in a hobby, or to highlight an organization or cause, then your tools should match the efforts of your focus. A well-thought-out plan can save your headache in the future.

Equipment, and even production value is important but there is something greater. Content is of the greatest value. There are so many ways to start yourself off in the right direction with equipment without it making your wallet scream!

Back in the 1980's the U.S. Pentagon came under fire in a procurement scandal. It was said that among the outrageous wasteful spending was found a hammer. It was the kind that you or I would pick up at a hardware store for under ten bucks. The government reportedly spent $500.00! Wasteful spending and over equipping your efforts is as useless as spending $500 on a $10 hammer.

Decide what your starting budget is. Determine what your monthly budget will be. With the advancement of technology and the ease of access to free online resources, you may already have everything you need to get started with very little initial investment.

You should also consider that within your budget there may need to be room for online subscriptions, web hosts, or podcast hosting. With your time being precious and the learning curve great, you might put your budget towards full-service production companies that can do a lot of the heavy lifting for you.

In the following chapter I will lay out considerations for equipment. I encourage you to connect with us at www.findyourvoice.fun . There, I will have information, classes, and interviews with experts in many areas of broadcasting, including the latest and greatest in broadcasting equipment. We will provide money-saving or free ways to get your voice out there.

9

EQUIPMENT 101

Imagine a sound studio with noise proofed glassed rooms, a control board lit up with buttons, slides, and meters. Equipment can be intricate but broken down, there are only five fundamental things that are needed to broadcast. Your basic requirements are a way to speak , record , listen , edit , and upload . These make up the outline of any broadcast set up. Speak, record, listen, edit, upload. Thus, your basic tools could be a microphone, headphones, or speakers, recording device, software program or app.

You can start broadcasting right away to an account on a social media or video sharing site directly from your smart phone. Anchor by Spotify, for example, is a free app that allows you to create, distribute and even monetize a podcast. Recording to apps is nearly as easy as making a phone call. Though creating a truly quality broadcast requires a bit more than a phone can provide.

For slightly more advanced productions, ear buds and a USB mic plugged directly into a phone or device can work with impressive results. Better sound quality can come with a step up the techno ladder with a professional XLR microphone, an audio interface, mic boom and shock mount, spit guard, a mixer, and editing software. A professional set up can include any number of newfangled, geeked-out toys, the sky is the limit.

I'll provide a basic run-down of the five broadcasting needs. You'll get an inside look at the specifics of my broadcasting equipment. Many of these items are available at www.findyourvoice.fun .

MICROPHONES

A quick rundown of microphones starts with the bottom rung. These are the built-in mics that reside in your computer, cell phone, or portable device. They are convenient but not suited for high quality sound. Camera technology in cell phones has drastically improved but sound technology has not kept pace. With the onslaught of amateur broadcasters, that might change quickly in the coming years.

The next rung on the microphone ladder is the USB microphone. These will connect directly to your computer through a USB connection. USB stands for universal serial bus. It is an industry standard for cable connectors. USB mics provide a decent sound quality.

As we take a few steps from USB mics, we find Dynamic microphones. Dyna mics enhance vocals and filter out other noises. Finally, the top tier of microphones is the condenser. This type sounds the most natural, nuanced, full, and rich.

NEXT LEVEL YOUR CELL PHONE

Microphones are used for converting sound waves into an electric signal for amplification, transmission, and recording. Technology is making quality microphones easy to acquire. Top notch gear from a decade ago was also bulky and price prohibitive. Digital cameras, handheld recorders, microphones are now programed right into your hand-held devices. While not as pristine in quality as an upgraded microphone, I have used my cell phone on location, in a pinch, for on-the-spot interviews, making recordings, and for broadcasting live on the radio. However, they do not provide that rich in-studio sound.

There are nifty little products that can boost your portable sound devices for better broadcast results. External mics plug directly into your phone delivering next level sound. There are condenser microphones which capture audio nuances. There are stereo microphones and digital XLR interfaces for mobile devices. These are tools that take what most of us already have and turn them into portable sound studios.

USB MICS

USB are standard on most all modern computers and devices. Many have multiple USB ports for a plug and play type connection. USB mics can have amazing sound quality. Technology has blossomed in recent years. When doing remote broadcasts, I have used a Blue Snowball™ USB MIC that is under $100 and loved it. You can find a link for this device at www.findyourvoice.fun .

XLR MICS

When quality is a must, high quality XLR condenser microphones are your best bet. This is what I use in my studio set up. XLR is defined as X (a connector), L (locking, the connector locks into place), R (rubber insulated). It is industry standard in the professional realm.

These mics transmit a nicely balanced, clean sounding audio. XLR mics types provide an omni-directional reception, which picks up sound from all sides. Or they provide a uni-directional reception, which picks up the majority of sound from directly in front of the mic. My XLR is uni-directional. It gives me a crystal clear, rich sound from me, yet it limits external sounds from around me.

AUDIO INTERFACE

My rounded, three-pronged plug on my XLR mic, unfortunately, does not connect directly into a computer. The solution is a high-quality interface. Computers utilize a sound card that acts like a translator, turning sound into data. The sound card is part of the computer's hardware.

An audio interface is an external sound card. It is a piece of hardware that connects to the computer. It allows you to join your microphones, headphones, and sometimes other devices to the computer. The higher the quality of the sound card or audio interface, the better overall sound you'll achieve.

Think of it like you would your senses. Your five senses are an interface between the information on this page and your brain that wants to consume the information. If you read this book, your eyes act as an interface to your brain. If you feel by brail, your sense of touch is the interface. If listening to an audio book, the interface is your ears. The sense of sound connects your brain with information like an audio interface connects the information from your microphone to your computer.

My microphones connect to my computer via audio interface. My audio interface also gives me added perks like manual sound adjustments for microphone and headphone volume. Interfaces can have many other features like the ability to add other sound sources. For me, Focusrite™ interfaces and Rodecaster™ have been spectacular.

HEADPHONES

You can get really fancy with 'blinged' out, ergonomically correct, cordless, noise cancelling headphones. Some people use headphone/mic combinations (though the microphone quality is rarely as good as corded mics). For me, simple studio monitoring headphones work just fine. On the road, I use ear buds.

I love to hear everything going on in the studio and on air. Headphones feel like audio claustrophobia to me, it's a personal thing. Because of my unidirectional microphone, I can set up my monitors to play in the background undetectable to the recording.

My philosophy is that quality sound is important, it can make or break a show's professional appeal. However, sound must be set up before the show and tweaked after the show in editing. During the show my focus is on giving my audience quality content. Having a technician that can manipulate things while you are on air is fantastic, but few people have that luxury.

COMPUTER SET UP

In my studio, I have a dedicated desktop computer, one laptop, five monitors, a tablet, audio interface, and an external hard drive for storing my shows and elements. When Covid forced many areas of the nation into lockdown, I had to suddenly find a way to do a drive-time terrestrial radio broadcast in a major market from my downstairs office in my townhome.

The radio station that I worked at sent me home with a "portable" suitcase sized contraption that connected me to the station through a modem. It was complicated and it would sometimes drop the broadcast during the show. I found that a well-equipped desktop computer and inexpensive and often free software worked so much better.

It was a bit of a nightmare finding just the right set up. I was very blessed to have my own professional technician, engineer, and computer software specialist that set me in the right direction and held my hand while getting things just right. But the reality that the means to professionally broadcast is available to anyone is astounding.

If you can connect with a crew of professionals, hire a full-service team, or utilize an established set up, good on you! Most people do not have access to a team of pros. Most just want to be certain that they are headed in the right direction. That is one of the purposes of this book. I will share with you the elements and equipment that I swear by, so you don't have the headache moments that I did or experience quite the same steep learning curve. You will also find tutorials, a master class, videos, and more at www.findyourvoice.fun.

10

NEXT LEVEL EQUIPMENT

As we look at the wonders of space exploration and man's improbable venture into the cosmos, it leaves us astonished at the machinery, engineering, mathematics, and sheer brilliance. Man has pushed through seemingly impassable barriers. He has set a trajectory through the universe.

Yet when man first went to the moon in the 1960's, pocket calculators did not exist. The Apollo guidance computer is said to have had only 36K of RAM and 2K of ROM. It weighed about seventy pounds. It didn't even have the capacity that your cell phone has today. Equipment is glorious and technology makes communicating to the world easy and accessible. But in the end, you can do the unimaginable even when you have less to work with.

If you geek out on cool software, digital upgrades, and are up on the latest equipment, you can find extraordinary resources for recording, editing, sound input, and whatever else you might dream up for your production. It can, however, be daunting for those not in the know. Setting things up for broadcast and learning how to use your setup takes time and sometimes help.

My setup took quite a while to tweak to near perfection for my purposes. I'm not entirely sure that I will ever be finished making adjustments here and there. There are always new products to try, programs to download, and updates to everything I use. I will take you on a tour of my professional home studio to give you insight into what a broad-cast set up can look like.

MIXING BOARD

A mixing board is a control panel that brings your audio (and some-times video) together. It has controls for adjusting volume and aspects of the sounds. You will see big mixing boards with sliding controls and knobs at every radio, television station, and sound recording studio in the world.

Today, you can find mixing boards that are virtual. They exist only as a program on your computer. I've used a mixing board called 'Voice Meter', from VB Audio. The Voice Meter board brings together sounds from my microphones, callers, guests, music, and sound effects from my computer and other devices. With it I can mix all sounds and send them out to my chosen destination(s). The Voice Meter is free for very basic use. You can pay more for more features. You will find this digital audio technology at www.VB-audio.com .

I also use a Rodecaster™ Pro interface as a mixing board. This extraor-dinary piece of equipment has everything I need and more in one slick professional-looking unit. It is a broadcasting studio the size of a small briefcase at a reasonably affordable price.

The Rodecaster™ Pro unit is an all-in-one podcast studio that will provide sound effects, bring in calls, connect with blue tooth, and more. It can record to an SD card and / or transmit right to a computer for use in any application. It automatically improves sound quality, lets you record phone calls, has convenient adjustments for sound, and hosts four microphone and headphone jacks.

The Rodecaster™ may be cost prohibitive if this is not a money-making venture for you, but the price is certainly not outlandish. At roughly $700, there is no piece of equipment that can compare. You can find it at www.findyourvoice.fun . Keep in mind that there are many less expensive alternatives that can start you out. It is always wise to work within your means and upgrade later.

Mixing the right balance of sound is an art. You may have the best equipment known to man at your fingertips, but the end result of balancing your elements still relies on you. There are some helpful tips of the trade that can start you out.

PRO TIP: The first rule of thumb is to watch your volume so that your sound, vocals, and music never over peak. If your monitors have a 'red' zone (red zone being when your sound levels reach beyond their maximum and become over modulated), your sound is usually best when it flirts with that red zone line but never quite crosses it for more than the briefest of moments. Keep your music as a bed below your vocal audio, never let them compete, unless it is purposeful.

SOUND EFFECTS

I play sound at the touch of a button. Many broadcasters have sound boards whose face looks like a scrabble™ game board with multiple buttons to press for any number of pre-programmed sounds, ads, and promos. As technology has advanced, these boards can also be found in virtual form within aps on your computer.

As a radio talk show host, I have used dozens of sound board programs and twice as many pieces of equipment. Having sound easily accessible is fundamental. It may be your opening introduction with a 'Big Voice Guy' and music. It can be news stories, videos, or sound effects. A sound board makes broadcasting and adding elements simple.

I will recommend three sources for sound boards. One is a piece of equipment, already mentioned, and the others are virtual software. The first is the Rodecaster™. The Rodecaster Pro™ not only has many colorful programable physical buttons for instant sound but also acts as an audio interface for seamless integration.

The other alternatives I use as well, Touch Portal from www.Discord.com . It is a downloaded application on my computer. It plays sound on from the computer and provides virtual buttons that are set up on a separate device such as a tablet or cell phone. The buttons can play sound, stop sound, play audio. These buttons can also be programed to do nearly any function I would want my computer to do at a press of a button. It can open a URL page, open a file, even send messages on social media. For my setup, I use it primarily to play and manipulate sound bites while broadcasting. Touch Portal's basic service is free for a limited number of buttons. I pay a premium for more options. The final option is from www.myinstants.com . It is a free site with programable sound bite buttons.

RECORDING AND EDITING

There is nothing that is more hair-pulling frustrating than recording a spectacular interview with an A-list, hard to schedule guest and then finding that something went wrong with the recording! I'm getting agitated thinking about it. Yes, it has happened once or twice to me before. To avoid this, I have multiple recording outlets and options.

My first recording outlet is 'Audacity'. It is a free, open-source, cross-platform audio software. I have worked at top-tier broadcasting studios that use Adobe Audition™ and other expensive software for recording and editing audio. Those software options are often best used for music production. Audacity is one of the easiest software programs to use for sound, particularly for talk formats.

Audacity is an easy to use, multi-track recorder and editor in which you can add your voice, record sound bites from websites, adjust sound or add effects. You can change speed, volume, layer tracks, and much, much more. It is compatible for Windows, MacOS, GNU/Linux and other operating systems. It is one of my favorite tools. There are other options that many will recommend like GarageBand, Hindenburg, or Pro Tools.

I will often do video and audio interviews via Zoom. Zoom has a free service. It gives me audio and video from my guests, allows guests to share pictures and audio as well. I can adjust the sound from my soundboard, and I can record Zoom interviews to either my computer or the cloud. By recording to the cloud, it gives me a recording option outside of my computer to fall back on in case something goes wrong.

There are numerous sites that provide recording, limited editing, and posting ability directly from your browser. Many podcast hosting sites will offer recording options. An online search will afford you a wealth of choices.

You can mix, record, and post using programs like OBS Studio (Open Broadcaster Software). www.obsproject.com is a free open-sourced cross-platform streaming and recording program. OBS allows me to bring together my audio, video, effects, pictures, text, etc. and then records them to my computer. It can also broadcast my production live to any number of social media sites and video sharing sites.

To get content to the most sites from a single effort I have OBS send my feed to www.restream.io . With this online service, Restream can record and broadcast your efforts or it takes a live feed from OBS and sends it to numerous social media and video sharing sites. You can sign up with Restream for free and are allowed a limited number of sites that you can share at no cost. With a monthly fee you can get extra platforms, stream recorded content, and gain other helpful features.

For recording capability and the easiest and most amazing post-production editing, my favorite tool also has a free plan and an upgrade option. Descript, at www.Descript.com , allows you to upload audio and video. Descript will also allow you to record directly and publish your work right from the app. It will instantly transcribe your project, list speakers, can show their picture each time they speak, and it allows you to edit video easily by highlighting and deleting text or using their editing tools. The results are seamless.

Descript can automatically take out filler words like, 'um' and 'uh.' You can tweak the volume, add additional pictures, and features. You then publish the finished project, download it to your computer, even embed a video with transcription to your website. I have found it to be the easiest program for editing I have ever used. It does just about everything I need and provides a transcript to boot. Additionally, their customer service has been amazing.

Finally, I do subscribe to a podcast hosting site and a web hosting site. The podcast hosting site posts my shows and will distribute them to the major podcasting sites like Apple, Google, and others. I use Podbean at www.podbean.com .

Many people choose full-service hosting sites. For a fee they will help you create, record, edit, produce, and distribute your show. It is the busy person's personal producer and well worth the cost.

WEB CAMS

Most computers come equipped with a camera for pictures and for recording. The quality is fairly good for computers produced in the last 5 years. I use an external Logitech Brio Webcam. The Logitech suite of products have downloadable programs that can help you to manipulate the picture and other brilliant broadcasting tweaks.

ADDITIONAL TOOLS

We have a layout of equipment vetted on our website. There you will find XLR microphones, mic-booms, spit guards, and much of the equipment included in this book. Whatever the job, pick the right tools. There are many fabulous options out there. Technology has made it easy for all of us to share our voice. I advise you to remember that while the right tools are important, the job or message is what it is ultimately all about.

11

LEARN THE STEPS

Belly dancing in our society has a sultry and somewhat sensual appeal. The beaded costumes, flowing veils, and distinctive core movements hold an exotic alure. Yet the roots of this dance style are based less on sensual expression and more on celebration.

What we know as belly dance is known as Rak Sharqi or dance of the East. It is an over 6,000 years old movement and a dance of, by, and for women. When men battled in wars, hunted for food, or scouted out new areas to conquest, women in their down times would make music and dance. It was the "girls just want to have fun" moment of the ancient world.

Mommas, aunties, and grandmothers used these movements to show younger women the movements of living. The dance trained their bodies for procreating, birthing, recovery, and staying well in older phases of life. Not unlike a yoga, aerobics, or Zumba class in our century, women gathered to stay fit for life in brutal times.

When a tribe was conquered and the men slaughtered, women would be carted away as the prizes of war. With them came their customs and their dances. This is how the traditions of the dance of the East spread. Romani Gypsies picked up the movements and shared them as they traveled.

With each new area came new appropriation and the addition of local flair. Today, belly dance is still a dance of women and of fusion. It has been fused with ballet, cabaret, hula, tap, and so many other forms of movement. Yet in every iteration there are familiar fundamentals. You will always find distinctive steps and movements that are the same today as they were so many thousands of years ago.

The purpose of this book is to help you share your unique message and impart to you the knowledge that I have mastered in the realm of broadcasting so that you can share your voice like a well-choreographed dance with the world. Your movements may be fused with your unique culture, but the fundamentals will always remain the same.

Your foundation is set, and the stage is laid. Your purpose is sure, your audience is pegged, and your hardware and software may be getting set up. Now, like studying the choreography of a dance, we can learn the steps that will make your efforts come to life.

You may be writing a blog, giving a speech, doing an interview, or starting a podcast. Having an outline for your efforts gives you structure and provides a sort of map to help you get to where you want to go. A well thought out outline, like dance steps, gives assurance to your audience. It gives them exactly what they deserve, your best.

The basic outline of every effort is the basic outline of your message. Learn this well. It will be the difference between a so-so production and a spectacular program. The outline format should always be hook , story , lesson , ask . These, sandwiched between an introduction and conclusion, create a skeleton for your communication projects to be fleshed out upon. What each of these elements will end up looking like, sounding like, and how they play out makes your broadcast as unique as your own individual dance.

INTRODUCTION

Your introduction sets the mood for what is to follow. For a video production you might include music, lights, effects, an announcer, or just you and any combination of these add-ons. Your intro must be impactful but always brief!

Someone recently asked me to monitor their podcast for consultation. Their program was twenty minutes in duration. I strained to figure out what they were about or who they were talking to. Though their introduction was well over five minutes and lacked focus, purpose, and brevity. It is the equivalent of going into a restaurant, having the waiter greet you but never give you a menu and never serving your meal.

An introduction is where you draw your audience in. It tells your audience who you are and what to expect. You can set the stage for your audience with what you are wearing, the tone of your voice, the music you play. Is this a high-level professional encounter? Is it casual and fun? Are you presenting yourself as relatable? An introduction is your first impression and is vitally important.

What about sound? Will this include music? Is your music copywritten and do you have permission to use it? Will you have a professional announcer? Perhaps you elicit a friend with a great voice or hire a voice actor. Will you use effects?

Your introduction will set the stage for what is to come. Use your introduction to hook your audience. Tease what your broadcast or conversation will be about. Show your audience your energy and give them something to whet their appetite. Never, ever let your intro be dull, boring, too long, or dry. You have an important message, and it deserves a vibrant start. In short, your introduction should be a welcome that addresses who you are, what your show is, and what your audience can expect.

HOOK

A hook is what draws a person in. The hook attracts your unique audience like bait on a fishing line. Dangle the right bait, and you will catch the right fish. It is because the hook is something that interests your audience. Your hook phrase meets your audience in a conversation or concern that they are already having in their head or heart. You are making a promise that their concern will be met.

Your hook is a simple, short sentence, or very short paragraph that tells your audience what you will do for them in this program and how they will find what they are looking for in your message. Your hook can be a formula of "If you (think, need, or feel) _____ then today we will

_____."

STORY

"If history were taught in the form of stories, it would never be forgotten," says Rudyard Kipling, Author of The Jungle Book. [1] If your voice is expressed in story your audience will not easily forget. It may be a first, second, or third-person account. It may be recited in news stories or played in sound or video clips. Your story may also include a dialogue or interviews. This element is vital to creating interest, driving home your lesson, and building engagement. Stories can be long or quickly expressed and come in endless forms, but no message is complete without them.

One of America's greatest story tellers was broadcasting legend Paul Harvey. Harvey took the news stories of the day, seamlessly interwove them with real people and their stories, and added commentary. He spun them together like a master wordsmith into Paul Harvey News and The Rest of the Story. He was carried on 1,200 radio stations, in 300 newspapers, and on nearly 400 American Forces Network stations. His fame centered around his ability to flow from news to tales and talk in flawless storytelling form.

Upon his death in 2009, the New York Times posted an obituary written by Robert D. McFadden. It gives a fitting description of what a true storyteller does. "[He] personalized the radio news with his ... opinions but laced them with his own trademarks: a hypnotic timbre, extended pauses for effect, heart-warming tales of average Americans and folksy observations that evoked the heartland, family values and the old-fashioned plain talk one heard around the dinner table on Sunday." [2] Harvey infused every broadcast with superpower elements through storytelling.

Your outline will not be complete without a well thought out, but brief, story. A story brings life to your points, opinions, information, and inspiration. You enhance your outline with story by bringing the main point to life through illustration.

If you are being interviewed, have at least three short stories at the ready.

Format them to illustrate important points. Bring all the superpowers of communication to life as your employ these intriguing tales. If you are a broadcaster, decide who will be the storyteller. Will you pull a tale or an illustration out of a guest, a news report, a sound bite, or from your own experience?

LESSON

The lesson in your outline is a statement, a conclusion. It is a moral to the story. Some have called it an "ah ha" moment. The lesson connects the dots of your story and gives your audience what they were assured of in your hook.

Your hook makes a promise. It tells your audience what you are going to do for them. Your story does it for them. Your lesson shows them how you delivered as promised. You can give this revelation with simple phrases like, "...and this is the point." "Here's what you should never forget." "This is what you can learn from this."

ASK

The ask is what puts the lesson into action. It gives your audience something to do with the glorious gems of information and revelation that you've opened like a treasure trove before them. It is both a call to action for your audience and a funnel that can drive your audience to an act that benefits you.

Let's say Joe Giggly, the daddy comedian turned podcaster, did a show giving fathers advice on how to talk to their daughter about their first crush. Dads share stories about how they embarrassed their daughters, said the wrong thing, or scared the living daylights out of potential suitors. Yet, somehow, their bumbling efforts made their daughters feel loved and protected. These were the stories. The lesson may be, "Remember that you will sometimes get it wrong, but love covers a multitude of sins."

The ask helps give your audience something to do with what they have heard. For Joe's audience it might be, "Whatever you do, right or wrong, tell your daughters you love them today." He may give them additional resources for more assistance.

The ask should also bring benefit to Joe's efforts. He might advise listeners to subscribe, join his mailing list for updates, listen next time for more, or become a partner to support his endeavors.

When someone has invested their time, and received benefit, they crave an opportunity to put it into action. It is like a payoff on their investment. It gives them a stake in the game.

OUT

Putting out an ask and then moving to your program's closing is your transition to your "out". Your out can be as simple as a "Thank you for listening." It can be accompanied by music, an announcement, or a tease for upcoming programs. Your out should be a way of ending your presentation and engaging with your audience through appreciation of their time. The out is also a perfect place to employ branding, like your logo or tag line.

The superpowers of communication are interwoven into these mysterious outline elements of communication choreography. The hook aligns with the engager, the story with the entertainer, the lesson with the informer, and the ask with the inspirer. Thus, these elements do more than just give you a clear, concise message. It infuses all the elements of a successful message into your dance.

[1] Kipling, R., 1941. The collected works of Rudyard Kipling ... [Garden City, N.Y.]: Doubleday, Doran, & Co.
[2] McFadden, Robert D. (March 2, 2009). "Paul Harvey, Homespun Radio Voice of Middle America, Is Dead at 90". The New York Times.

12

FINDING CONTENT

Their church building had been viciously vandalized by radicals more than a half-dozen times. Set on fire, windows broken, doors beaten down, a skeleton structure was all that remained. The parishioners were brutalized and threatened. Their resolve, however, remained unshaken as they resorted to meeting in a semi-secret location behind their shattered chapel.

Each Sunday, the old and the young, the well, and infirmed would walk up to ten miles for their gathering. They traversed their way up the red dirt mountain path that snaked its way behind the remains of their church building. A cart of fruits and goods was placed by the road to make it look as though people were simply gathering for a small market, lest they draw the ire of those opposed to their faith.

It was deep in the tropical interior of Java Island, in the country of Indonesia, on Paseban mountain. We were on a humanitarian outreach to meet these resilient people. The country, the language, the risks, the customs, were quite foreign to me. Tasked with speaking on this trip, I wondered how I would find content, connection, and common ground.

As we ascended the pathway to their gathering, a familiar sound reached my soul. The words were in Indonesian, but the tune was a hymn that I had sung since my youth, "How Great Thou Art." The message was clear, though the lyrics were not.

We gathered on mats on the dirt floor. The pieced together shack was almost completely hidden within the rich vegetation. There, our translators conveyed the stories of the persecuted.

We took in the depth of their poverty, noting that in anticipation of our visit each attendee wore their very best. Even their best was tattered and holed. We ate together, as we brought food to share. They had little but the women still prepared for us a small cake of sticky sweet rice decorated with vibrant local flowers.

I spoke almost no Indonesian but wrote a simple song to share my heart. Rita, a local, was their song leader. She and I shared smiles, hugs, and harmony. As we left Rita pulled me aside, hugging me like a dear friend. Then, looking me in the eye, she pulled her scarf adorned in an intricate batik pattern indigenous to the region from her neck. She placed it in my hands with a loving smile. I tried to refuse. How could I take something from her knowing she has so little? But with her eyes welling up, she wrapped it around my neck, touching my face. Without words, her message was loud and clear. If we were born in another place and time, I am certain we would be close friends.

The point is that I lacked the oral communication skills to speak to these beautiful people, I was at a deficit. Somehow I still, however, I made an impact. Be encouraged; every communicator, broadcaster, or writer can grapple with finding content. Remember that there is no end of resources for communicating your passion. The music, the food, the smiles on this trip were as much a message as a great speech. Sometimes you just need to look beyond your normal. Sense the needs of your audience. Nurture your passion. Find inspiration in ways you may not have anticipated. Above all, always be the true genuine you, speaking your true genuine heart.!

The following are elements you may use to infuse your coffers with content. These are places to which you can look for inspiration, good stories, and ideas. If your resourcefulness is running dry, revisit these components, get recharged. Then return with a revitalized message.

TRENDS

Follow trends. Search out popular subjects. keep up on breaking news and issues that fascinate your audience. These are ways to secure a continual flow of inspiration for any communication effort.

There are innovative ways to keep these ideas flowing in. Check out Google trends to view trending searches. Examine hash tag popularity. Explore topics that are at the forefront of people's minds.

GROUPS

Join groups on social media. Find groups that align with your passion and message and allow your fellow members to become a type of associate producer. They will post interesting thoughts, share stories, and trending items. You can appropriate these ideas, turning them into content.

SUBCRIBE

Subscribe to newsletters, periodicals, and web sites that feed your interests. If the content moves you, it might move your audience. Finding topics for your efforts is a balance between what interests you and what your ideal listener wants to hear.

NEWS

News stories provide a constant flow of content with the hard work of content, creation, writing, and formatting being done by someone else. News is powerful as it can unite people through experience and bring a current relevance to topics that you wish to present.

When we share news that is pertinent to our passions, we connect our audience with others whose interest was piqued as well. News stories give examples for our lessons and add interest to our broadcast.

Take note, however, the way news is reported and used has changed drastically over the last few decades. Inflammatory, unconfirmed, or spin doctored content that shocks an audience is the rule of the day. For the sake of credibility and professionalism take the high ground.

The Radio Television Digital News Association (RTDNA) is "the world's largest professional organization devoted exclusively to broadcast and digital journalism. Founded as a grassroots organization in 1946, RTDNA's mission is to promote and protect responsible journalism." [1]

The RTDNA, in its code of ethics, says that "Journalism's obligation is to the public. Journalism places the public's interests ahead of commercial, political, and personal interests. Journalism empowers viewers, listeners, and readers to make more informed decisions for themselves; it does not tell people what to believe or how to feel." [2]

It may seem that news outlets violate their own code of ethics in daily reporting. Those violations break trust and can destroy credibility. According to a Gallup poll, trust in the media is at an extremely low point with only 7% of U.S. adults saying that they have "a great deal" of trust in the media as of 2021.

A professional approach to sharing news and separating news from commentary will bolster your credibility. There can be a place for hearsay, speculation, and rumors, but in journalism, truth and accuracy are paramount. If you cannot confirm a report by trustworthy means, either do not use the story or honestly tell your audience that this story is reported as-is, reportedly took place, or is unconfirmed. Make a distinction between the news story and your own point of view. True news is unbiased.

COMMENTS

Check out the comments sections. When you read news stories that are pertinent to your message scroll down. There are often comments listed below. In these comments is the heart of those who were motivated by the story. Here is where you can find a treasure trove of content.

QUESTIONS

Your purpose is powerful when you meet the needs of your audience by answering a question they are already asking. Pay attention to the FAQs of web sites. If you can address these, you have an effective coffer of ideas.

GET TOGETHER

Attend events, gatherings, and conferences that run congruent to your message. Here you can connect with others passionate about similar topics. You can meet potential guests or contributors and collect ideas.

Truth be told, no matter the flow of content, sometimes you will simply burn out. There will be times when you just don't have the words or the enthusiasm to communicate. In these times it is perfectly fine to give yourself a break. Take time to recharge. Reconnect with things that motivate you. Re-find your passion.

The poor population of church goers in the Paseban mountains of Indonesia found motivation in the face of persecution. When it would be easy to give up, they found respite in the very things that most moved their souls. In the face of oppression, they reconnected and continued. They are my motivation to fight the good fight and to keep sharing my voice.

[1] Rtdna.org. 2021. About RTDNA and RTDNF. [online] Available at: https://www.rtdna.org/content/about_rtdna [Accessed 4 October 2021].
[2] IBID

13

THE TRUTH ABOUT PUBLIC SPEAKING

Where, just three days prior, a basketball game played out before a booming crowd of fans, I stood surrounded by thousands of participants in a much bigger game. It was my first political state convention. National figures, movers, and shakers, along with famous names graced the stage of the massive arena.

Booths adorned in red, white, and blue decor were hawking bumper stickers and tee shirts. They were butted up against tables hawking policy, positions, and political candidates. Lined up in row upon row they sprawled in this seemingly endless field of faces. Standing alone, I took it all in.

A hand on my shoulder and a familiar voice jarred me. John was his name. He and his wife were two of the most beautiful people I have ever met. They were passionate and brimming with integrity. What a delight to see them participate in political affairs where some of these traits can be wanting.

John shared his desire to be a delegate. Delegates are chosen to represent their state party at the national nomination of the President of the United States. A delegate is officially nominated by an attending individual and then elected by vote. I told John that I would be delighted if he would allow me to be the one to officially nominate him before the gathering.

Mark Twain once said, "There are only two types of speakers in the world, the nervous and the liars". You could almost feel the angst of the speakers. Like a massive wave, it emanated from their nervous words, as they stood there before peering eyes. Their voices quivering and timid, they looked down at the paper held in their hands to anchor themselves. They stated their business and left the stage quickly thereafter. One woman, I recall, nervously held the podium so tightly that she broke off a piece of its wooden frame.

It has been reported that at least 75% of humans fall victim to some sort of angst when speaking in front of people at one time or another. It can range from slight jitters, a bit of nervousness, to full-on panic. Some might call it stage fright.

The fear of public speaking is the most common of human anxieties; it is said to out rank even the fear of death. In its full-on phobic mode, it is known as glossophobia. Increased blood pressure, dry mouth, a sensation of tongue swelling, body heat and perspiration, muscle stiffening, even nausea, are what many suffer. Though one in four people will experience some level of public speaking apprehension, fearfulness need not prevent the effective sharing of one's voice.

As I approached center stage of the convention, I felt like a tiny speck on a massive stage, in an immense stadium, before the largest gathering of people I had ever experienced. Of the tens of thousands in attendance, there could not have been more than a handful of people truly paying attention. Most had zoned out long before I trekked up to the microphone to speak. Determined that my efforts would not go unnoticed, I employed all that I knew of the art of public speaking. What happened next was astounding.

Taking a cleansing breath, and with every ounce of confidence I could muster, I took a moment. Then I smiled. In my best, 'on air voice,' I started slow and low, building in enthusiasm. "Ladies and gentlemen can I have your attention please! (Pause) I am Michelle Mendoza, and I am about to share with you a nomination that will inspire your hope in America!" To my astonishment, my confidence hushed the entire arena. I surprised myself by continuing to speak when I wanted to stop and just shake my head, 'seriously?!' As I went on to share the virtues of my nominee, I could see people in the stands hushing others as they strained to listen. With sincerity and certainty, I gave my brief spiel to the raucous applause of the gathering.

Many others crossed that stage, both before and after me. Their nominations may have been just as worthy and integrous as my friend John, but they were without the enthusiastic response that somehow my short speech garnered. Ineffective communication skills and anxiety in public speaking dampened their efficacy.

Is there a difference between jumping out of the path of a speeding car and speaking in front of a group of people? Psychology Today says, "no." "Our fear of standing up in front of a group and talking is so great that we fear it more than death." [1] More than death?! "The fight or flight response activates complex bodily changes to protect us... We need to respond without debating whether to jump out of the way of on oncoming car while in an intersection...The threat area of the brain can't distinguish between these threats." [2] Public speaking or deadly threat, your brain often cannot tell the difference.

Comedian Jerry Seinfeld put it this way, "More people are terrified of making a speech than dying. That means most people at a funeral would rather be in the coffin than giving the eulogy." What if speaking trepidation is hindering you? What if it keeps you from success?

Fear and lack of public speaking skill leads has profound consequences. Would you like to lose 10% of your monthly wages? How would you like a 15% reduction in your chance of promotion? These are the results of a lackluster presentation. Additionally, 96% of people believe that communication in the businesses that they deal with daily needs improvement. According to Salesforce , a customer relationship management platform, 86% of employees and executives blame workplace failure on ineffective communication. So even if you feel confident in your abilities, it never hurts to improve your communication skills.

If every human has a level of public speaking fear, and yet people do it every day, there must be a trick to mastering that fear. Fear need not define you. Trepidation need not hinder. The secret is in being prepared. No more than 14 years old, I was invited to spend a warm summer day in a ski boat on the lake. An older teen drove the boat and I, somehow, had to be the first to put on skis and jump on in.

I had never water-skied before. None of us really knew what we were doing. I bobbed in the water, awaiting my fate when the boat yanked suddenly. I jerked forward, slamming face first into the water.

My diaphragm frozen, I was breathless, and unable to move. If not for the floatation device I wore, I would not have been able to keep my head above water. In that moment I was terrified. As the air returned to my lungs and the boat returned for me, I realized the folly in doing something dangerous with no instruction, preparation, or know-how.

It makes perfect sense to have at least a twinge of unsurety before speaking. Like putting on water skis with no instruction, you do your best, and try not to drown. If you are not prepared, trained, or coached, you could fail.

The next time I put on skis, I was older and wiser. I did not let the fear of past failure paralyze me, but I did not go in without help. Still a little nervous, I listened carefully to instructions. I watched others who knew exactly what they were doing. I asked questions.

Perhaps my performance was not that of a world class water ski champion, but I did stay up on my skis long enough to completely enjoy the experience. Whether skiing on a lake or speaking before a convention of thousands, fear is fear. With tips, training, and preparation, our experiences can become better with each experience.

[1] Croston Ph.D., Glenn. "The Thing We Fear More Than Death". Psychology Today, 2021, https://www.psychologytoday.com/us/blog/the-real-story-risk/201211/the-thing-we-fear-more-death.

[2] Montopoli, J., 2021. PUBLIC SPEAKING ANX-IETY AND FEAR OF BRAIN FREEZES - National Social

Anxiety Center. [online] National Social Anxiety Center. Available at: <https://nationalsocialanxietycenter.com/2017/02/20/public-speaking-and-fear-of-brain-freezes/> [Accessed 27 October 2021].

14

BEFORE YOU SPEAK

Bridezilla! In preparation for her big day, the bride demanded that her guests dress be very specific. That is if they were of a certain acceptable weight. If they were heavier, they were ordered to wear black or camouflage so they would not be as noticeable. Awkward!

When the public got hold of the story, the backlash was brutal. The bride backtracked. She then instructed guests to instead prepare to submit to a polygraph test to reveal who leaked the story.

In the same vein, another bride demanded that bridesmaids do mandatory weigh-ins. They were not permitted to be thinner than the bride nor to cut or color their hair without express permission. There have been brides that wouldn't allow their bridesmaids to wear makeup so they would not outshine the bride. Or those who demanded chemotherapy patients to wear a wig or stay home. The pressure of perfection can bring out the worst.

You might experience a simple courthouse nuptial or, conversely, a lavish destination wedding. You might be giving a short toast at a reception, or a long-involved speech before an auditorium packed with people. With the right planning and reasonable expectations, your efforts need not turn you into a stressed-out perfectionist monster.

Public speaking like weddings of any size take planning. Your masterful public address starts long before you take to the microphone. You may have weeks to prepare, or you may have just been tapped at the last minute to speak off-the-cuff. The preparation for any presentation is still the same.

OUTLINE

Outlining your effort provides you with a roadmap of where you are verbally headed. If you lose your way, your outline will direct you back on course. Your first order of business is to determine your destination or your main point, your lesson. Where do you want to take your audience?

Next, like making a travel itinerary, determine how you will lead your audience to that point. It makes no difference if you are giving a short 30 second introduction or a long presentation. Just as if you were getting in your car and planning a trip to the grocery store or a cross-country trek, you still must know your route.

Utilize the hook , story , lesson , and ask . The hook meets the audience where they are at. It draws them in with something they need. It says, "This is what I'm going to do for you." Your story is the human-interest portion that gives relatability and illustration to your point. The lesson is the meat, the main dish, of the presentation, it offers that main point. The ask inspires your audience to action.

In that state convention I spoke at, my speech was short and simple. See if you can identify the hook, story, lesson and ask.

"Ladies and gentlemen can I have your attention please! (intro) I am Michelle Mendoza, and I am about to share with you a nomination that will inspire your hope in America! (hook) The first time the words to our national anthem came to life to me was on a 4th of July, sitting by the bank of a river, watching fireworks as a teen. The rocket's red glare and bombs bursting in air made me cry. I realized just how blessed I am to have this liberty and what price was paid for it. (story) If you understand that level of gratitude, then you can appreciate people like John who earned a Purple Heart defending that freedom. He continued the fight, as a man of color, supporting integration and understanding, working toward mending differences in our communities. He still seeks to serve our nation, and you, today, as a delegate. (lesson) Please join me in a round of applause of thanks and please give your support to John as a delegate to the national convention. (ask) Thank you. (out)"

NOTE IT

Notes, like crutches, can hold you up. They steady and support you as you verbally walk through your presentation. You cannot, however, run effectively when using crutches.

Notes work best when they are no more than bullet points. An over reliance on notes makes presentations less relatable and less sincere to your audience. Reading a speech at people is never as effective as speaking to people. The less time spent looking down at notes, the more engaging and effective your message.

The key is to be prepared then keep it simple. Before your address write out your speech, create PowerPoint slides, and research points. When it comes time to face your public simplify your notes by reducing your research down to its outline and bullet points.

You'll have four sections in your outline - hook, story, lesson, and ask. That's four bullet points. My bullets are followed by one simple word, or a very short sentence to prompt me. This becomes my road map.

Jump in your car for a drive to a friend's place. Put their address in a navigation app and listen for step-by-step directions. The app's friendly voice may say, "In 100 feet turn left onto 72 nd St." This short and concise instruction gets you to where you need to go with minimal distraction.

If the voice laid out extraneous instructions in paragraph form, you would likely miss your turn. Imagine, "As you continue to drive in your vehicle, in about 100 feet, you will need to get into the left turn lane on the road that you are driving on right now. You will then turn left onto a street that goes by the name of 72 nd St." You can see how that just doesn't work.

The same applies to speaking. Think of your outline as your step-by-step directions to get you through your talk. Simple and concise will direct you best.

EMOTIONALLY PREPARE

Skydiving or giving a presentation, both can cause anxiety. Offset trepidation with preparation. Anxiety means you are human. Yet emotionally preparing for any event can grant confidence. In that confidence anxiety can turn into enthusiasm.

Unlike the danger of falling from the sky, hoping your parachute will open, giving a less than adequate performance on stage will not likely cost you your life. In fact, as we have discussed in the book FIND YOUR VOICE Your Superpower and Passion Unleashed, your imperfections make you relatable to an audience. There is something inspirational in watching someone that is human and even fallible succeed in delivering an inspiring message right before your eyes. Much of the success starts with a firm foundation of preparation.

Once you have your speech, your notes, your bullet points, and perspective right, you then have a foundation. Remembering that you possess a superpower and a super voice, use this opportunity as your moment to shine. Take a minute to bask in that surety and let it replace angst with enthusiasm.

BREATHE

Adrenalin takes over. Our air passages dilate. Oxygen is forced away from our brain and into our body. Our muscles can shake. Suddenly we are in freeze, fight, or flight mode. In this condition many have found the strength to survive and achieve superhuman feats. It can cause us to do things we would never think we were capable of.

"A 19-year-old teen named Charlotte Heffelmire not only lifted a burning truck off of her father, but she also saved her entire family from a fiery fate. Her father Eric was working on his car in the garage when the jack slipped, pinning him beneath the vehicle, but that wasn't all. The impact of the car falling onto him caused gasoline to spill, it ignited all around the garage. Charlotte rushed into the garage and tried lifting the truck from her father. Charlotte (said), "I lifted it the first time, he said 'OK, you almost got it,' finally managed to get it out, it was some crazy strength, and pulled him out." Examples of Charlotte's type of sudden weightlifting ability have also been coined as "hysterical strength". [1]

As you rise to the stage before you, there is really no need for super strength, heightened ability to flee, or the need to pull a body from underneath a truck. When adrenalin hits it has the side effect of causing your muscles to twitch and shake from excess energy. Oxygen rushes to your body and unfortunately away from your brain. That makes it difficult to give a thought provoking or inspirational speech. That is why it is vital to 'just breathe.'

A few minutes before a public address, performance, appearance, or anything that causes a little anxiety, breathe. Pushing oxygen through your system, calming your nerves, and reoxygenating your brain will give you peace and focus. Concentrate on the points of your speech.

Breathing Exercise:

Try this exercise. Relax your tongue on the roof of your mouth. Breathe in through your nose for a count of five. Make it a slow breath, aiming the air towards the bottom and back of your throat. Breathe that air deep into your diaphragm as though you are filling your stomach with air. Keep it in for a count of five. Exhale through your mouth with a hush sound in a count of five. Then sit still for a count of five before starting the process again.

This amazing exercise pushes oxygen through your system and to your brain. It will quell nerves, anxiety, stress, anger. It will help get you ready to perform.

It makes little difference if your presentation is long and you've had months to prepare or if you are asked to give an off-the-cuff talk. Take at least a moment to choose your destination. Map out a hook, story, lesson, ask. Lay out bullet points. Breath. Prepared, outlined, bullet pointed, and breathing easy, you are ready to broadcast your voice.

[1] PACELLA, S., 2021. 15 Times Adrenaline Took Over And Turned People Into Superhumans. [online] https://www.therichest.com/. Available at: <https://www.linkedin.com/in/sara-pacella> [Accessed 13 November 2021].

15

YOU'RE ONLY AS GOOD AS YOU SOUND

As he enters the spaceship, all who behold him tremble in fear. He may be the most iconic villain of all time. The black helmet, face mask, and cape, breathing apparatus that produced the disturbing raspy breath, and of course his deep ominous voice, made Darth Vader top of the bad guy list. Vader came onto the collective scene in 1975 when Star Wars first hit theaters. He was voiced by James Earl Jones, but few knew that the physical actor was a man named David Prowse.

Prowse had a commanding presence as a strongman, body builder, and weightlifter, standing at six-foot six-inches tall. He mastered the physical role of Darth Vader but is said to have complained bitterly that his voice was dubbed over for the film. His angst reportedly got him banned from future films and from Star Wars conventions.

Classically trained actor James Earl Jones was tasked with voicing the menacing villain. There are recordings of the original uncut filming with Prowse's voice barely audible behind the Vader mask. It seems weak and common when matched to the chilling and powerful vocals of Jones. Darth Vader could be a maleficent rogue but with the wrong voice, it is hard to take him as seriously.

While sharing your voice, never let your vocals impede your power. While you do not need to sound like James Earl Jones, learning the techniques of professional communicators will help your message to be palatable, respectable, and powerful.

During interviews, speeches, or audio only broadcasts, your voice will give that all-important first impression. When in person or on video, a professional appearance that matches your message will let your audience know what you're about and if you should be taken seriously. So too, how you sound and how you use your voice will turn your audience toward or away from your message.

I will share with you ten steps to a better voice performance. Walk through these daily to become the best vocal version of yourself. No matter your level of vocal experience, training yourself to use your voice like a fine instrument will improve your message and help you to have a greater impact on your audience.

10 STEPS TO BETTER VOCALS

HYDRATE

We naturally dehydrate when nervous or performing tasks. Alcohol, coffee, and not drinking enough water are also common ways we dry ourselves out. Talking can leave you parched as well. Being in the midst of a performance with a dry coughing fit is more than frustrating.

Your vocal cords need moisture. They are comprised of layers of membrane that vibrate as you force air through them, producing sound. They can shorten and lengthen to create pitch. To do this amazing task they must be pliable and hydrated. Hydration not only helps to produce sound but will protect your voice from injury and keep your brain focused as you speak.

Make hydration part of your daily routine. Have water, or water with a bit of lemon on hand when you are talking. The lemon can clear out any rattling phlegm hanging out in your throat. The water can keep you sharp and your voice powerful.

RELAX

When speaking, particularly in public, it is common to tense up. Our shoulders will rise, and our body tenses up. Our vocal cords strain and our voice can shrill. Conversely, when first getting up in the morning, still groggy and wiping sleep from blurry eyes, our voice is markedly rich and deep. This is because we just stirred from seven hours of relaxation. A deeper tone in your voice commands an authoritative presence. It comes from a more relaxed state and creates a more relaxed feeling in your audience. Studies have shown that a deeper tone in communication results in a greater feeling of trust and interest.

Before speaking, relax your entire body. Massage your neck and shoulders, roll your neck, calm your muscles. Shake out your stress.

Take a few moments before you speak for a 30 second vacation. To reduce stress and encourage normal breathing, you might take your mind on a short get away to somewhere peaceful. Close your eyes, choose a destination, see, smell, and experience your surroundings. This tricks your brain and body into disconnecting from the current stress and resets your mental system.

BREATH

Learning breath control can greatly improve your vocal performance. Proper breathing can help quell nerves and sharpen thoughts. You can gain volume control and energy with the right breathing techniques.

To get your body into proper vocal breathing mode, try this exercise. Imagine holding a tennis ball in your hand. Open your mouth and pretend to stick it in as though you're going to swallow it whole. As it rests in your throat try to breathe around it. This exercise will help you naturally belly-breathe or breathe into your diaphragm.

Another helpful warm up just before speaking is the dry laugh technique. Simply practice a deep belly laugh without making any sound. This process will warm the diaphragm muscles getting you ready for breath-controlled vocals.

Your diaphragm gives power to your words. Breathing from it naturally lowers your tone. It can give you more control over your vocals. Train yourself to breathe from your diaphragm when speaking.

STRETCH

Your voice needs to get ready for performance like an athlete would prepare before a game. A professional baller would never go into a soccer match without stretching. You should not go into your performance or interview without preparing.

Start with stretching and preparing your face. Try this small to big stretch. Make your face as tiny as possible. Purse your lips, close your eyes tight. Then make it as big as possible with a wide-open mouth and great big eyes. Hold each pose for five seconds and repeat at least five times.

Try the cow cud stretch for your tongue. Move your mouth like a cow chewing cud or if you had a gigantic wad of bubble gum in your mouth. Make sure your tongue is getting into the action. Loosen your face and mouth and get ready to communicate.

EXERCISE

Next, we will work out the actual voice. Before a singer takes to the stage, they do a series of vocal exercises that increase range and sound. Warming up the vocal cords also prevents damage to your voice. Vocalizing is a physical process. Like working out for the rest of your body, healthy exercise makes for a healthy voice.

To help increase your range and work on your lower register, try this exercise. Start to hum. Hum in a high tone and feel the vibration just under the chin. Move your tone lower, feel it in your throat. Continue going lower and moving your hand down your body as you go. When you find your lowest note, linger. Hum louder and longer. As you raise both hands above your head, your power should seem to increase. Next, move from the hum to an "ahh". Say, "Maw, maw, maw."

Conversely, run your voice up the scale. Use the phrase, "My mom made me mash my m and ms." With each word try to raise the tone just slightly. These exercises will get your voice ready to use.

DENASAL-IZE

High pitched nasal voices leave the audience with a sense of anxiety. They are widely held as unpleasant and off-putting. Studies show that messages delivered from a nasaled presentation are not taken as seriously. It would be a shame to have a dynamic message that no one hears because your nose gets in the way.

Hyper nasal speech is caused by too much air going through the canals of your nose as you speak. Check your nasal level by holding your nose with your thumb and pointer finger just below the bridge. Then say this phrase, "The bell rang." You should feel almost no vibration with, "The bell," and vibration on "rang." Experiment with your lower register until you master the right vibration.

DYNAMISIZE

When playing a musical instrument, you will hit high and low notes. You will play fast and you will play slow. Each note and each pace have purpose. Any song would be quite boring if it played only one note at the same pace. Your voice is an instrument. Utilize the high, low, fast, slow, stop, go method to enliven your delivery.

High tones and fast speaking should be used sparingly. They denote enthusiasm and excitement. They can encourage and enliven, but over-played, can be stressful and hard to follow. Low tones convey confidence and authority. Slow words bring points home and a purposeful pause gives the audience a chance to catch up and digest what was said.

Bringing the highs, lows, fast, slows, stops and go's together brings dynamics to your presentation. Your voice becomes interesting. The presentation becomes easy to follow. Your voice, like a song, hits a portion of your listener's brains that makes them remember your words and ingrains them into their world.

EMOTIONALIZE

Your presentation must have those four magic elements of entertainment, information, inspiration, and engagement. The engagement is the emotive element. When you bring it alive in your presentation you create a connection with your audience.

You can easily infuse emotion into your presentation by using and bringing alive emotive words. When there is a word that you can infuse with emotion, do it with just a touch of description in your voice. The word freezing can be said with a tense shaking voice. The word hug can be said with warmth. Smile when speaking of something positive. Be cold and intense when speaking on serious matters.

To develop this emotive trait, read children's books. Bring them alive with description in your voice. Remember when speaking to adults to tone it back, a little goes a long way.

ARTICULATE

The last thing you want to do is sound like a mumbling teenager with a bad attitude. Instead, use bright, crisp enunciation. Make your words clear and understandable. The result is an audience that perceives you as intelligent and reliable.

A technique that many broadcasters use is the tongue twister. To loosen the tongue and encourage proper pronunciation, look up a list of tongue twisters. Read them as quickly as you can. Over articulate, exaggerate the words, over pronounce the letters. Then you'll be less likely to get tongue tied when you are live.

Here are three common tongue twisters

Peter Piper picked a peck of pickled peppers. A peck of pickled peppers Peter Piper picked.   If Peter Piper picked a peck of pickled peppers, where's the peck of pickled peppers Peter Piper picked?

How much wood would a woodchuck chuck if a woodchuck could chuck wood? He would chuck, he would, as much as he could, and chuck as much wood as a woodchuck would if a woodchuck could chuck wood.

She sells seashells by the seashore.

READ

Practice putting all these steps into practice by reading aloud. Listen to yourself as you read. Tweak your approach. Record yourself and listen back with a discriminate ear.

KEEP IT UP

If you think of your voice as an instrument you can put into perspective the effort needed to train it to sound professional. There are casual guitarists who know a few chords and play simple songs by a campfire and there are classical experts whose fingers fly over the strings, producing music that wows. We have all played our voice all our lives but mastering it like a fine instrument can take your effectiveness to a new level.

16

AS YOU SPEAK

Meet Nick. Without medical explanation or warning, Nick Vujicic was born without arms and legs. He struggled much of his growing up with depression and loneliness. He wondered why he was different and if his life truly had value. Nick's faith gave him the purpose he was searching for and at the age of 19 he began a speaking journey that has taken him around the world. He has since shared his story in filled stadiums to millions.

Nick founded an international ministry, Life Without Limbs. Their moto is, "If God can use a man without arms and legs to be His hands and feet, then He will certainly use any willing heart!" And I would contend that any willing voice can be used to make a difference as well.

It does not take "perfection" to deliver a perfect message. Nick has come a long way since his first public address at age 19. With the right tools and growth, your voice can change the world.

Now it is the moment that you have been preparing for. You have found your foundation and inspiration. You have tapped into your niche and discovered your superpowers. You have found your voice and developed its message. Now is your time to speak your voice to the waiting world.

How is it that some presentations sound polished, professional, and captivate the audience with entertainment, engagement, information, and inspiration? How do you know if your presentation will be good enough? There are secrets and processes that the best public speakers use to magnify their message's efficacy.

YOUR POSTURE

First impressions are everything. If you stand on the stage schlumped like a timid child, your audience will respond accordingly. Chin up, shoulders back, a smile, and look of confidence in your eyes will inspire confidence in what you are about to present.

As you stand before your audience take just a moment to connect. If you were to open the door to your home and welcome these folks in, what should your facial expression look like? Take this moment to look over the crowd, your podcast host or guest, or the camera and smile as though you are looking directly at your audience avitar. Take one more deep breath and begin.

EYE CONTACT

Just as looking down at notes repels an audience, eye contact connects. Yet, it is a tricky thing. If you have been in a crowd and a speaker makes prolonged eye contact with you, it can make you feel uncomfortable. Brief contact connects without discomfort.

One way to give the appearance of connection is to look just over the heads of your audience, changing your focal point every few seconds. If you need to look down at your notes, try not to break the mood. Do this by keeping your facial expression consistent.

PRO TIP: Here's a trick for adding a spectacular advantage to your audio efforts for broadcast. Find a picture of someone that represents your ideal listener, reader, follower. When you broadcast, make eye contact with that picture as though speaking to them. I promise you it will add a level of connection that you can be proud of.

SPEAK TO THE BACK OF THE ROOM

The last person in the last row is as important as the guy sitting directly in front of you. While yelling will not endear you to anyone, a strong, sure voice will invoke a sense of self-assurance. Your audience will then naturally follow your words with confidence. Even if you are aided by a sound system and microphones, communicating as though you are including the person in the back brings your audience together.

SLOW DOWN

It is quite natural, as you stand before peering eyes or in a broadcast, to speak at a faster pace. Your voice will rise in pitch and your breathing will become shallow. From your very first word, purpose to speak low and slow.

Slowing your roll gives you more control. It aids in enunciation, so that your words are clear and crisp. It gives your listener a better chance at understanding your message. The slowdown method will transform your speaking power and give your words more weight.

PURPOSEFUL PAUSING

Silence may sometimes be golden. Pausing for effect allows your listener to catch up, to ponder, and to take in the points of your message. Repeating an important phrase or portion of your message has a similar effect. In the times that you lose your focus or find yourself grasping for your next point, do yourself a favor. Pause with purpose.

Do not 'break character.' Breaking character is a theatrical term describing what takes place when an actor in a performance is playing a character then suddenly stops acting as their character would. This can in turn break connection with the audience. In a speaking engagement or an on-air broadcast do not break the moment by breaking character. Use the moment to stand in confidence, smile assuredly, and pause. You might repeat your last statement, which can often get you back on track. Find your place with your bullet points. Then begin speaking again all without breaking character or changing your expression.

SMILE

If you do lose your way, if you feel the twinge of nerves coming upon you, smile. Take a moment to give an honest, genuine, 'I care', smile. A smile relieves stress and tricks your body into elevating its mood. Smiling, in turn, helps your audience to relax and feel at ease. It endears you to them and gives a feeling of well-being to all. When all is said, and your words are done, finish your talk with a grateful smile.

These simple practices can make an immeasurable difference. Practice makes perfect. Before a mirror or in front of trusted friends, practice these tools of the communication trade. Like learning to ride a bike, the first time you might be shaky. The experience need not be miserable. As you continue you will improve with each opportunity.

There is nary a human being that can escape the platform of public communication. From job interviews, business connections, customer service interactions, to taking marriage vows before friends and family, communication is at the heart of our involvement in society. The 38 th president of the United States, Gerald R. Ford, once said, "You can speak well if your tongue can deliver the message of your heart." If all else fails, remember that at the heart of your words is your passion, your voice.

17

LET'S TALK INTERVIEWS

Grey skies surrendered a constant drizzle across the dampened landscape. The dripping beads of rain created river-like patterns across my windowpane. Another inside play day. This was indicative of much of my growing up in the Greater Seattle area. A portion of the country known for long, soggy, rainy winter weeks.

Perhaps it was not so long ago, yet a scene from another time and era. It was just before online connections, a world without computer apps. The terms tablet and face time meant something completely different than they do today. You wouldn't find a child inside on a rainy day glued to a computer screen.

With technology a few years from its inevitable explosion, cell phones were not in the hands of every child. There was only one piece of technology, the "social media" of the day, that young girls, like me, would flock to. It was the push button, analog telephone, attached to a wall jack. The only resemblance it had to a mobile phone was its long, long cord that enabled you to walk about the house, though still tethered.

Times were different but the need for childhood gossip was not. I would find myself on weekends bound to the telephone, my parents following the cord's length to see where I had holed up. Inevitably I would be lying on my back, feet up against a wall, listening to music, and chatting with Haggy, my best friend. My parents would eventually have to force me off the phone. It wasn't hard, all you had to do was pull the plug.

In this current time in history, we have a need to pull the plug. Cell phone addiction has turned society into walking zombies with everyone looking down at their phones as they mill about. We see it in restaurants with families dining together yet each on their own device. On average we check our smartphones over 150 times per day. We're always online but are we truly present and connected?

"Two in five Americans report that they sometimes or always feel their social relationships are not meaningful, and one in five say they feel lonely or socially isolated. The lack of connection can have life threatening consequences, said Brigham Young University professor Julianne Holt-Lunstad, who testified before the U.S. Senate in April 2017." [1]

This is why friendship, love, and even interview formats are vital. Interviews are intimate by nature. They are the most genuine form of broadcast communication.

Consumers listen to or view interviews as a single participant. An interview thus becomes a cozy meeting of the interviewer, the interviewee, and a listener. An interview conducted well will grant an audience a meaningful connection in a time of emotional disconnect. Done right, you can be a profound connection in a vacuous world.

Connections and communication seemed to come much easier when we were kids when we were full of expressive play and imaginative interactions. Where did that voice go? As children, our voices spoke out with more freedom and less reserve.

I recall riding my bike to the neighborhood park. There you would play with children you knew and some you did not know and may and may not ever see again.

Social norms, rules of conduct, and a loss of childhood wonder grow us up. The pressures of life stifle the once free flowing dreams and vibrancy that guided youthful communication. Gone but not forgotten. This type of free-flowing connection is key to a glorious interview.

Do you remember that feeling of being welcomed at the playground by the band of unfamiliar children? You watched longingly as their little fists turned white from grasping the rails of the hurling merry-go-round. You waited your turn; you wanted to play. Your desire was simple; you just wished to join in the fun. You may have stood by tentatively, awaiting the moment that you would be welcomed in. Then, suddenly, you were all friends, and the fun began. That is much like the feeling of being the audience, or guest on someone else's show. Like walking into playtime in progress, the guest and the audience need to be part of the fun.

A good host's job is to bring everyone into the game. A good guest will jump in, like the new kid on the field ready to knock it out of the park. Together they can reach out a hand to the audience to connect them to the action. Believe me, this is magic for your efforts!

In my experience it takes about ninety seconds for a guest to ease into the interview fun. That is if the host is like the child that makes the new kid feel like they are welcome. If the host lacks that skill, a wise guest will employ the superpowers of communication to elevate the broadcast and connect themselves with the audience.

In the first moments of an interview, you set the stage for the rest of the interaction. In those first moments, your counterpart will know if this is going to be a stiff awkward experience or a genuine and engaging one. They will almost always respond accordingly. You are in charge of the playfield and the game is about to begin.

PITCHING A GREAT GAME

Drawing people in, connecting them, how does this happen? You can liken an interview to pitching a baseball. Employing your skill and directing the message of an interview is much like the ball's projection. It should go exactly where you want it to.

The ceremonial 'first pitch' of a baseball game is thrown out by a celebrity of sorts. Love him or hate him, in 2020, the first pitch of the season in the Major League Baseball game between the New York Yankees and the Washington Nationals was thrown out by Anthony Fauci, head of the U.S. National Institute of Allergy and Infectious Diseases. He was also the front man of the disastrous Covid 19 issue in the United States that year.

The New York Post cited Fauci's pitch as #1 in a list of 'The 11 worst first pitches ever...,' saying "...(Fauci) wound up and hurled the ball just a bit – OK a lot – outside. Fauci threw up his hands in a shrug as Sean Doolittle (pitcher for the Nationals) chased after the ball, a fitting opening to an abnormal season." [2]

Interviews, like a pitch, require talent, developed skill, training, practice and good execution so that you and your audience do not end up shrugging your shoulders and trying to figure out where things went wrong.

The recipient of your pitch or message, like a catcher, should sense that you know what you are doing. You do not have to be a major league expert to give a good pitch, but you do need to be prepared.

For those who are being interviewed, knowing the process and being a good guest is important to your success. You can simplify this into four things. Be true to your passion, focus on your audience avatar, make your host look good, and always employ the communication superpowers through your hook, story, lesson, and ask.

[1] Official web site of the U.S. Health Resources & Services Administration. 2021. The "Loneliness Epidemic". [online] Available at: <https://www.hrsa.gov/enews/past-issues/2019/january-17/loneliness-epidemic> [Accessed 13 October 2021].

[2] Walker, M., 2021. The 11 worst first pitches ever: Fauci, 50 cent and more. [online] Nypost.com. Available at: <https://nypost.com/list/worst-first-pitches-ever/> [Accessed 22 September 2021].

18

PITCHING A GOOD INTERVIEW

It was a stifling hot Sunday afternoon at baseball's League Park. Nearly 20,000 fans packed the stands on this late August day in 1919 to watch the Cleveland Indians battle the Philadelphia Athletics. It turned out to be much more than just another day at the park.

Clear skies during the first pitch gave way to sprinkles, sprinkles, by the final innings, surrendered to ominous skies. In the final moments of the last inning, angry clouds began to swirl, the skies grew darker, and heavy showers pummeled the field.

With just one more out to secure the 2-1 win for the Indians, pitcher Ray Caldwell, known as "Slim," faced off against shortstop "Jumping Joe Dugan". Suddenly the sky seemed to burst open as fierce lightning bolted through the stadium. Electricity sizzled across the stands, and it was said that the diamond seemed to be set on fire. Players buckled to the ground but poor slim was knocked flat on his back.

Staff and players began to assess the damage, still jittering from the event. They realized that Slim was lying motionless on the mound. It was tragic. As fans made their way back to their seats, a stunned hush fell over the stadium.

Suddenly, a breath and movement. Ray "Slim" Caldwell somehow survived the strike. As one of his teammates reached out to help him, they were nearly overcome by the crackling electricity Slim was emitting. In this one story for the history books, Slim brushed himself off, pitched the last ball, and won the game!

In the game of broadcasting anything can happen. Interviews can take an unpredictable turn. Even after a near death lightning strike, Ray Caldwell, shaken and sore, relied on the fundamentals of his craft to win the game. You are about to learn interview fundamental secrets that will get you through any eventuality.

The fundamentals of a powerful interview are much like pitching a baseball. A pitcher kicking the brown dirt of the mound beneath his cleats knows that there are five basic phases to hurling that ball like a pro. There is the wind up, the cocking phase, acceleration, deceleration, and follow through of a pitch. An interview, like throwing that baseball, follows that pattern.

PITCHING PHASES OF BASEBALL AND INTERVIEWS
THE WIND UP

In the wind-up phase of baseball, the pitcher establishes what kind of pitch he or she is going to throw. They determine where it is going to go, and how hard or fast it's going to fly.

In an interview, determine the particulars of your interview by researching the person you will be speaking with, the topic, and their angle. Establish what kind of interview you are going to do. Determine the direction that you want the interview to go. This is your wind-up phase.

Part of this wind-up is a dive into your guest or host. Know about whom you will speak with, their life, their projects, their angle, and their style of conversation. Gauge if you can, their communication superpower so you can draw on it or supplement where they are weak.

Develop a basic understanding of the subject matter, relevant news items, and what your conversation might offer both your audience and theirs. You do NOT have to have their life's works memorized but you should not be ignorant of it either. When we know too much, we tend to run out of great questions to ask. Have your outline and a list of possible questions, answers, and stories ready. Now you have your wind-up.

THE COCKING PHASE

The cocking phase is the beginning of the real action. This is where the pitcher transfers energy to generate velocity. For an interview, it is where you transfer your energy to your hook. Here you will state what is about to take place. Give your audience something fantastic to expect.

This cocking phase is vital for your counterpart. It gives them an understanding of where you are going to take them. They can metaphorically hold out their gloved hands like a catcher behind home plate ready to take the heat. Communicate through your words, mannerisms, and attitude what kind of person they are going to engage with. When you are in an interview, remember you are on the same team as the person you are speaking with. You don't want to catch your "catcher" by surprise. They should know what you are going to throw at them.

THE ACCELERATION

Acceleration is the stage where energy explodes. The action of acceleration is powerful when you watch a pitcher in motion as they release the ball. For you this is where a host will pitch out a question or comment to the guest, and sometimes vice versa. The acceleration phase is an action stage that draws out the power of the interview.

Here the guest responds with an acceleration response. This is where they bring stories to life. In turn the host can nurture interesting anecdotes and information. This phase of the interview should be full-on entertaining and engaging for the broadcast. It conjures pictures, emotions, information, and connections in the mind.

Hosts will "accelerate" through strategic questions such as, "Tell me what happened?" "How did that make you feel?" "What did you think about that?" "What is something you'll never forget about that?" "Why is this so important?" "How does that work?"

Guests do not despair if these accelerating questions are not asked. You can always impart them for effect yourself, "Here's something I will never forget about this." "Here's how this works."

THE DECELERATION

The ball is barely out of the pitcher's hand. This, however, is not a passive phase of the pitch. For interviews it is the active listening stage where you observe, listen for cues, watch for connections. The deceleration phase is vital to success.

In the world of baseball pitching, deceleration is where most injuries in throwing occur. Likewise, in an interview, it can be where the worst mistakes are made. You can foul out if you are not engaged in this portion of the interview.

Pay attention to how your questions and comments are perceived. Are you really being understood? Are you drawing out fascinating and needed information? Are you making the broadcast shine? Evaluate if your counterpart is comfortable. Are they feeling awkward? Are you talking too much or not enough? Are you using your voice effectively? Center in on what they are saying and doing. Find ways that you can connect it to your next statement or question.

Deceleration success is tied to targeting. A pitcher targets the catcher, you target the audience. If you focus on them more than your own promotion, your message will be better received. Hosts, help your guest by asking questions that your audience would ask. Guests, following your host's lead, they will connect with you, your ideas, and their audience. This phase is all about connection.

One of the many rainy-day games our family played was Dominos. In the game of Dominos, you have 28 tiles with spots on both ends of each tile. Players take turns connecting the dominos and matching the dots, until someone is out of tiles.

Deceleration is an engaging and connecting part of an interview. It is like matching the domino dots. What is being said should get you thinking about how to match up the next idea, follow up, comment, or story. You can think about the connection of where the conversation is going, how to add value to it, and where you want to take it. This is where your broadcast emits a professional flow.

THE FOLLOW THROUGH

In baseball pitches, after the ball is released, the pitcher's body continues in motion. Follow-through is an integral part of accuracy. In broadcast interviews, your follow through is an effective "follow up". You have been actively listening, formulating what you might do next. Now you pick your domino. Connect the dots. Put your thoughts into words with your follow up comment or question.

Your follow through ensures that the ball goes where it needs to. It travels with your intended direction and impact. In the interview, you up the ante by supplementing comments, observation, purposeful pauses. You can reinstate an important point and titillate your audience's imagination.

TIRED ARMS & WILD PITCHES

Every pitcher has the occasional tired arm or wild pitches. Even in winning seasons, there are games you'll win and some you'll lose. Don't let those bad days and poor pitches be a reason for you to throw in your glove. Listen to your broadcast with a critical ear, take note, tweak things. Re-evaluate, learn from your mistakes, and grow. Some of the most common issues are easy to train yourself out of.

Beware of wandering. Some speakers have a hard time giving up their moments in the spotlight. Some are impassioned but lack the focus to stay on track. They wander off topic and so does the broadcast. The more focused the more successful your efforts.

Beware of rambling. Learn to self-regulate. Let your counterpart talk. You will always sound better when you talk in sound bites. Beware of boredom. Pay attention to your responses, your questions, your stories. Use the magic of the four superpowers of communication to bring your part of the interview alive.

Baseball is a beloved part of American culture. Its stories, history, its struggles, and victories enthrall. Your interviews can also enthrall your audience. You can titillate listener's imagination, which can beat out the best effects of any high budget Hollywood production. Where movies have limitations, no matter what the budget, a human mind does not. Your interview can stimulate, it can enrapture, it can engage your audience.

19

HOW TO GET INTERVIEWS

I remember recording interviews on old technology known as a tape recorder. My neighbor friend, Karen, could be seen running alongside me, holding the equipment like a professional grip. We interviewed my dad about his work on the Boeing 747 back in the day. We spoke with Karen's mom about what secret ingredient she added when making boxed mac-n-cheese that made it so delicious. We interviewed her dog, a spotted Dalmatian named Val. Val did not say much.

I do not think anyone from my childhood would be surprised that I was destined for a career in broadcasting, entertainment, and particularly a talk format. While there is so much that I have learned since my days of interviewing neighborhood canines, the childlike fascination, genuine interest, and real care for the subjects of my interview remains. My best advice for getting interviews is that if you keep your passion vibrant, your will draw vibrant interviews and you will vibrantly impassion your audience.

FINDING INTERVIEW OPPORTUNITY

For hosts and guests alike, networking is the beating heart of getting guests on your show or being a guest on someone else's. Everywhere you go and every connection you make could be a lead to your next great interview. Here are some outlets that are worthy of your attention.

ONLINE GROUPS

Social media holds connections within connections. There are specialized groups on every subject and interest that you can imagine. Type in key words pertinent to your message and a list of groups of like-minded people will appear before you. In these groups are interesting people, posts, quotes from experts, and people of interest. It is a smorgasbord of people that you can find, message, and connect with to either invite to be interviewed or ask to be interviewed by.

TRADE SHOWS AND CONVENTIONS

Trades shows, conventions, and places where potentially interested people gather can build your contact list. If someone is committed to paying an entrance fee and dedicating time because of an interest, they will also be interested in getting their money's worth. Good networking connections and interviews are a way to build value into their investment and yours.

Strike up conversations. Ask about their interests. Get inspiration from booths, speakers, and attendees. Compile your contacts and write out short notes then and there, before you forget. You can reference this list for contacts for your future efforts.

ORGANIZATIONS

If there are organizations, businesses, or charities that align with your passion contact them for interviews. Follow their blogs and any articles or books that they put out. Make your request relevant, professional, and concise.

COLLEAGUES

Network with friends and colleagues and not just the ones that have similar interests. The people around you may have a fresh and interesting perspective. Tossing out your passion at gatherings, around the office water cooler, or over coffee with friends may open you to innovative ideas and connections that you had never considered.

OTHER BROADCASTS

You may be looking to be interviewed. You have a story to tell; search out broadcasts whose audience resembles your target market. Prepare a powerful pitch of your message. Marry it with relevant news items or current events that are already playing in people's minds. Follow the hook, story, lesson, ask format and include possible questions. Always make the first paragraph of your pitch concise with all pertinent information. You can provide additional details afterwards if you wish. Include, along with your name, title, and contact information, a brief bio.

Broadcasters looking to grow their audience can benefit from an interview exchange on other like-minded programs. You have a niche that is specific to you. In that niche, you are not competing with other formats, you complement each other. Introduce your counterpart to your people and let them do the same.

PUBLICISTS

Publicists are experts at connecting and promoting. They work hard to make their client's work relevant, timely, and impactful. They often have a pitch list of broadcasters and publications connecting interviewees with interviewers.

If you are an author, podcaster, speaker, presenter, ministry, hiring a publicist can link you to broadcasters and their audience. Publicists expose you to new markets. There is a cost to hiring a publicist, pricing can vary. If you are monetizing your effort, a publicist may well be worth the hire.

For broadcasters, make sure that you are on publicists' list of contacts. Do an internet search for publicists. Research which would align with your efforts. Contact them, telling them about your program and ask to be put on their pitch list. Publicists thrive on building their reach for maximum impact for their clients. If you can provide a professional, high quality, reliable interview you will build a relationship with publicists. Keep these contacts happy with professional communication and follow through. It will be a benefit for the interviewer and the interviewee.

Learn to give a good interview. It makes it easier for your publicist to market you. It makes them look good and reflects well on your product. As a broadcaster it can make your job much easier as well. There is this enchanted place where you no longer must hunt and peck, beg, and hope for great interviews. After establishing relationships with organizations, publicists, promoters, broadcasters, and the like, they start to know you and come to you. Your email box will be brimming with glorious, ready for broadcast folks to interview. It takes time to nurture these relationships. Once you do, never take them for granted. They are your associate producers, so to speak.

MAKING CONTACT FOR INTERIVEWS

Whomever it is that you are enticing to the table, your contact request needs to be professional, appealing, informative, and please, please, make it concise. The contact email needs to represent you honestly, accurately, and most importantly, aim for giving your target something they need or desire.

What do you believe is the favorite topic of any guest or person? Without exception, it is themselves. Take a group photo then post it on social media. People will seek out and focus on themselves before others. Your potential contact has a voice and passion that they want to share. Research what they are most passionate about, what they seem to be driven by. Appeal to those aspects.

MUTUAL BENEFIT

Guests on talk shows are not typically paid money for their time but they should get something of value in return. An interview should include promotion for a book, a plug for a business, and a website mention. Some broadcasts will post their guest's picture or link on their website and in their show's description. When making contact make clear what it is that you wish to promote.

Guests also do not pay to be on a show. If you are paying to be on a talk show you are not a guest, you are an infomercial. Infomercials can be successful, but they can also come off as disingenuous.

TIMING

What about timing? As a guest it is best to leave times and dates of availability as open-ended as possible. You may have an event or time sensitive issue. You might have parameters for your best times or dates based on your schedule. Include these but keep in mind that you are asking to come to someone else's party. They have the right to decide when that party will be.

Many broadcasters ask me if it is presumptuous to request a set time and date when inviting a guest on their program. While it can be hard to gauge the schedule to others, in my experience I have found that if you leave the date and time open-ended, you have less of a chance of securing a booking. If you give a time, it can always be changed but you will more likely walk away with a commitment.

EXAMPLE CORRESPONDENCE FOR BROADCASTERS

Emails to interview prospects must give the guest enough information to prepare. If you are being queried, you know that an outlet that presents all pertinent information is organized and trustworthy. I've included an email query and request form that I have used for inviting guests. It is short and to the point. It tells who I am, what I do, and what I would like to do for my guest. This gives my potential guest everything that they need to know to do an interview with me.

EMAIL

Hello (NAME or REPRESENTATIVE),

I'm _____, host of _____. We would like to invite you to share your (book, podcast, organization, etc.) " _____" on an upcoming episode. Our listeners are people who are passionate about _____ and I would like to introduce them to the ideas that you share in your _____. Our show is broadcast on _____. Below, I have a suggested date & time, along with some particulars for our interview. Please let us know if we need to adjust the time for your schedule. You can find more about us at _____.

Thank you for your consideration. I look forward to our interview.

INTERVIEW REQUEST FORM

GUEST REQUESTED : (I use this line if I am contacting a promoter, publicist, organization, or manager.)

DATE : (suggested date of the interview)

TIME : (always, always, indicate the time zone. You can use your own, but it is better to utilize theirs if you know it.)

REACH : This will be a live-recorded interview. It will be syndicated and rebroadcast on dozens of venues. Including (list the platforms you post to and include video sites if you use them like YouTube, Rumble etc.)

TOPIC of the broadcast : (This is where you initially inform your guest of what you are going to talk about. It is the "What I'm going to say", portion of the invitation.)

TOPIC for guest : (list their book or organization and/or what information you want to discuss. You might list sample questions or ideas. These are best found from your potential guest's book, website, or writings.)

DURATION OF INTERVIEW : (your interview might be a short 15 minutes or a longer one. It is easy to schedule in a 30-minute segment for most people. The longer the duration, the harder it is to secure a time.)

HOW TO CONNECT: (if you want to phone them or have them phone in this is where you would state that. Will you connect via zoom or skype? Give specific instructions here.)

HOW TO REACH US: (make it easy for them to contact you via phone, email, or any other means)

SCHEDULING

For those seeking to be scheduled on a broadcast, I have found that the best pitches provide a great hook in the email subject line. Include in the body a name, title, short bio. This is followed by the hook, the answer, and ask. Tell them what you will do for them, what you have to say, what they and their audience will gain from it. Then provide pertinent contact information to make it happen.

Before you hit send, have a schedule dedicated to your efforts. Organize your interviews and broadcasting tasks. An online schedule is easily shared with others on your staff and those you will be broadcasting with.

I include in mine the name, title, and one sentence bio of whom I will be working with. If pertinent, the name of their book (with subtitle), movie, website, organization, or whatever claim to fame they have. I list the topic of the show, how we will connect, along with contact information. Including web links and appropriate news stories gives you everything you need in one easy to reach place.

FOLLOW UP

There is a sweet spot of timing for interview requests and follow up. Think of your schedule at its busiest, then imagine adding a 30-minute interview into it. You would want a reasonable heads-up for scheduling. So do your prospects. Conversely, if your heads-up is three months away, by that time, things, news, schedules can change.

I have found that about a one to two-and-a-half weeks' notice is right in that sweet spot. Hit there and you will have a better chance at getting a "Yes." Also, waiting about three days to follow up, if you have not heard back, gives your guest time to sort through emails and not feel like you are pestering them.

When a guest does turn you down or does not reply, unless they, in no uncertain terms, make it clear that they would rather die by the heat of 1000 burning suns than be on your show, I always leave the door open. I send a thank you, I'm sorry it did not work out this time perhaps we might find a better time/date that will work. Perhaps we can revisit the request at some time in the future.

Guests, remember that that is exactly what you are, a guest. If you are a guest in someone's house party you don't tell them that they must schedule the party at your convenience. You do not dictate what they serve. Be a gracious guest and you'll have better success.

GIVE THANKS

As a child, I could not begin to recall the countless times my mother would entreat me to say, "thank you". Sending a thank you after the broadcast is more than just good manners, it establishes you as someone who cares. If you are specific, all the better. Point out something special that you appreciated from the interview.

Another way for hosts to say thank you is to include a link to the interview. If you have the ability, send an embedded code for them to post the interview on their site. They can use these on their own media outlets. This is free marketing for your efforts!

ABOUT CALLERS

Callers are like mini-interview guests just of shorter duration. There are few things more vibrant to a broadcast than listeners/viewers interacting with you. Utilizing listener mail, commentary, or taking calls is one way to always keep your broadcast fresh.

In radio some call it "opening the phone lines". A live audience can deliver interesting questions with ease. It is energizing to the audience when they hear someone that represents them.

All productions require time to build up audience numbers to elicit calls from. Statistically, only about 1% of your audience will pony up and interact. If you are not live, you might invite those who have commented, emailed, or ask friends to join in.

Treat your callers like mini guests. Just as you have a voice and something important to share, so do they. It is your job to nurture that message to bring it out. Utilize the "pitching phases," from our baseball analogy, to help move the call along.

Interviews and being interviewed can be one of the most engaging aspects of communication. It is a way to promote your interests and enhance your audience's experience. I've come a long way since interviewing the neighborhood Dalmatian. The art to interviewing, getting interviews, and being interviewed is a journey. Where every you are on the voyage start with your passion and the people whose lives you seek to enhance.

20

START ME UP

If you have ever held a hand crank powered flashlight, you know that the more you turn the knob the brighter the light becomes. That's what it is like to share your voice. Your spectacular light shines brightest when cranked up with passion and preparation. Everything that we have addressed, thus far, has been to encourage you to find your voice and prepare you to share it. This is where you put dreams into action.

Thinking back to some of my first broadcasts, there was one unforgettable night. The radio station was mostly dark and barren. It was after midnight and only the studio was illuminated by the lights on the sound board and the flicker of numeric readings from the wall of transmitters. Only I and a friendly security guard, making his nightly rounds, occupied the grounds. It was just weeks into my first real job, on a real radio broadcast, on a real large market music station.

Newbies will often cut their teeth in the wee hours of late-night broadcasts. I worked weekend and midnight to 6AM shifts. My parents kept a listening vigil while I was on the air. My voice gave assurances that their girl was safe and well as they fell asleep to the music and messages of their nineteen-year-old daughter's broadcast.

Around 3AM, the dark broadcast room was suddenly illuminated. Sirens and flashing blue lights accompanied a floodlight that blinded me through my ground floor window. A squad car squealed to a halt. The security guard burst through the door, out of breath, and in a panic. He nearly unbolted the heavy soundproofed door in the process. The look of relief on his face fed into the mystery. What was going on?

My mother had awoken with no sound coming from their radio. From a dead sleep, the silence jolted her as she hovered over the bed, like a scene from a horror movie. She was screaming, "Dead air, dead air, dear God it's dead air!" Dead air is a term used in radio when there is nothing being broadcast, the music may have stopped, and nothing could be heard going out over the air. My mother rushed to the phone, calling the police. The police phoned the security desk at the business campus that the station was set in. Security moved into action to see what had happened to the young broadcaster.

As it turns out, my dad had awakened in the middle of the night. He did not like the song I was playing. He turned their radio off.

All the excitement took place just as a song was about to run out. In the mayhem I would have to get on the air and transition to the next song, tease it, give the time, station call letters, and be funny, interesting, or engaging, all in 10 seconds or less. No pressure.

I learned from my mentor that you must always go in prepared, but you must remember that you cannot prepare for everything. In chaos, never surrender to unprofessionalism. You, like a soldier under fire, must fall back on your training. My mentor taught me that when you are faced with something you cannot prepare for, there is no replacement for genuineness and confidence.

I got on the air with confidence, professionalism, and honesty. I told the audience that there were police just outside my window! "You won't believe why! I'll tell you more coming up, just after this song."

Monday morning my program director phoned me. He was blown away at how I had turned the situation into an on-air success. His phone blew up from listeners who said that they stayed up through the night to hear more from the feisty girl in the early hours of the morning. That day he gave me my own show. I have my mentor and a little disaster to thank.

The confidence in a well-prepared voice is obvious to all, even in unforeseen circumstances. If there were a natural emergency, like an earthquake, the most prepared individual will have the greatest chance to fare well in the chaos. Those who take the time to plan, pack an emergency kit, and discuss options with family will endure better than those who just react. When something happens, training and preparedness will pay off.

In broadcasting, you must have the confidence and ability to weather the most outlandish situations. Paying close attention to the lessons of this book, the companion book FIND YOUR VOICE: Your Superpower and Passion Unleashed, the classes and coaching at www.findyourvoice.fun will help you develop the confidence to navigate storms and not just simply react.

A few years after the dead air debacle, I experienced my very first time behind a microphone as a talk radio host. I filled in for a well-known personality. The topic was set and I felt woefully uneducated. Falling back on my mentor's advice of being as prepared as I could be, and where I could not, be authentic and honest. I did so with the audience. I prepared stories and items and asked them to phone in to educate me on what I may not know. They did and it astounded me.

I put into action the tenets of great interviews. I employed the superpowers of entertainment, engagement, information, and inspiration. Now I am sharing with you the secrets that worked for me.

LET'S GET STARTED

Your final step in preparing to launch is to do a few simulated broadcasts. Mock shows are where you put your plans into practice. Invite people that will enjoy being part of the preparation process. Arrange for friends to be callers.

Record your efforts. Listen back. Then edit, make notes, and tweak what you must. Listen like a listener, watch as a viewer. When you have your project where you want it, congratulations, you have your first show, speech, or broadcast.

SOUND CHECK

Like setting the stage for a band and making sure the audio elements are working properly, a broadcast sound check listens to your product so that you can pick out what is good, grow from what is wrong, and find ways to improve. The following are some basic things to watch for as you monitor your projects.

VERBAL CRUTCHES

"Uh, um, ya know, like," and other utterings are what we can fall back on when we are gathering thoughts or feel a need to fill the silence. We often just use these verbal crutches or filler words out of habit. It can be an annoyance to the audience and will make you sound novice.

We all use them, and it is not a show killer to have a crutch now and then but the fewer the better. The more you hear them in your replays the more it might make you cringe. Cringing will help you change the habit and clean up your broadcast.

BE THE AUDIENCE

It may make sense to you but does what you're presenting make sense to someone new to your broadcast? There are few better ways to lose someone than to confuse them. If you are unclear, or make your audience feel like they are not in the know, they will tune out. Listen to make sure that your efforts make sense and are obvious to whomever may be a witness.

LISTEN FOR QUALITY

Does your audio sound right? Is there balance? Are your music or sound bites fuzzy? Are there awkward sound moments? Does the room seem hollow? Will you need sound proofing or to move to a different location? Listen for these faux pas to boost the quality of your efforts.

BE YOUR OWN WORST CRITIC

Listen to your work. Do you sound robotic or unnatural? Are you engaging? Could you have asked better questions? Did you talk over someone? Did you talk too much or too little? Are you talking at rather than to your audience? Are you boring? You should always hear something in your broadcast that makes you take a step back. Without discomfort it is impossible to truly grow.

ENERGY CHECK

Does the show have oomph? If you find it dry or think it moves too slowly then your audience will as well, even more so. We can make the mistake of trying to put too much information into one program. That can overwhelm and lose an audience, stealing the energy from the show. The adage of "less is more" might be helpful where information is concerned.

For energy, too much can also be overwhelming. In concerts, a band will balance their playlist with upbeat and slower songs. If they do not change the energy just a little the monotony turns the audience off. Watch for the right energy and you will have better programs.

CREATE CREATE CREATE

If you are doing an initial launch of videos or a podcast it is recommended that you have at least three complete shows ready to post. Some venues will only allow you to post if you have at least three in the bag. I recommend five. This shows that you are serious about your program, but it is also an advantage to you.

If someone finds your video, post, or podcast, multiple shows tell them that this is not just a one off. People can come back for more. It establishes you, especially in an age of binge indulgence. In your five show, have at least two "evergreen shows" (shows that are fresh and not time sensitive). Evergreen shows can give you a nice back up if you are unable to produce a program for whatever reason.

If you are speaking in public, prepare three speeches and in each include at least one story for every point. Utilize the hook, story, lesson, ask format. Gear your speeches to different groups or interests within your target audience.

OTHER THINGS TO CONSIDER

Now you are on your way. You have at least a handful of programs, talks, broadcasts in hand. I once heard that for any broadcasting effort to succeed, it requires four things, product, permanence, promotion, and purpose.

Utilize the power of "permanence" or consistency. Your audience needs to know what kind of experience they will have when they connect with you. They need to know that you will be on the same venue, the same time and frequency, with the same basic format. Having a consistent brand, logo, music, creates a reliability that provides stability for growth.

Your efforts also require "promotion". What good is a broadcast, a lecture, a podcast, a show if there is no one to hear it? Remember the Beatles tune, " Eleanor Rigby"? "Father McKenzie Writing the words of a sermon that no one will hear." [1] In the song about lonely people, it reveals that, "no one comes near." "No one was saved." So what is the point if there is no audience? That is where marketing your voice comes in.

"Back to one," is a phrase used in filming. When a director uses it, the cast and crew resets the scene, going back to their original locations. Remembering that your voice has a purpose, is your, "Back to one." Recalling your purpose and calling can empower your journey. It helps to avoid burn out. The mental and physical effort of finding, preparing, and sharing your voice becomes a joy.

[1] Beatlesebooks.com. 2021. "Eleanor Rigby" by The Beatles. The in-depth story behind the songs of the Beatles. Recording History. Songwriting History. Song Structure and Style.. [online] Available at: <http://www.beatlesebooks.com/eleanor-rigby> [Accessed 17 October 2021].

21

MARKET YOUR VOICE

Crests were flown proudly, bannered above kilted clans who cheered on their best men in competition. Bagpipes played in a moaning legato, a rousing fiddle beckoned a Ceilidh dance. It was a warm early September celebration at the Scottish Highland Games.

It looked as though challengers were hugging telephone poles as they charged across the field in the caber toss. Josh wanted to compete for the MacMillan clan, but at the tender age of 12 he could only sit back and watch. His dad made him this promise, if Josh spoke like a Scotsman the whole day, he would give him some cash. He could buy a tee shirt with the family crest or some trinket to remember the day by.

Standing at a merchants table later in the afternoon, Josh and his dad eyed the sabers and Celtic daggers that laid before them. One long, wicked looking, scimitar caught his father's eye. He unsheathed the weapon and, as he did, the sun sparked ominously, like lightning, off of the blade. The sword in one hand and sheath in the other, Josh's dad sought to return the weapon back into the safety of its holster, but something happened.

The sharp point of the blade missed the sheath and penetrated deep into the palm of his hand! The sound of piercing flesh was audible to the small crowd that collectively gasped and was then suddenly hushed as the blade hit the table. Blood pooled and dripped with the beat of this father's pounding heart. Onlookers gathered to see the spectacle.

Then, out of the crowd arose a small figure. He lifted his hands to silence the murmurs. In a loud, powerful voice, feigning a very convincing Scottish accent, he spoke with a confidence beyond his years. It was Josh.

He cried out, "Ey don't you worry! We are MacMillans! That is but how we test our weapons to see if they're sharp, ya kin?! It is nothing but a butter knife, it didn't go all the way through!"

His father wrapped his wounds, as he and the entire crowd erupted in raucous laughter. Surrendering to the moment, Josh's father acquiesced. "Josh, my back pocket. Take the wallet, all the cash is yours, you earned it."

That moment resulted in an unintended consequence that we could call a marketing success for the sword merchant at that Highland fair booth. In the aftermath of the spectacle, an unexpected run on blades and baubles unfolded. The shopkeeper could hardly keep up with the frenzy. One man asked, "How much for this anyway?" as he picked up the still bloodied scimitar. The excitement even drew in passersby who had not been privy to the cause of the rush.

Marketing, as defined by the American Marketing Association is, "...the activity, set of institutions, and processes for creating, communicating, delivering, and exchanging offerings that have value for customers, clients, partners, and society at large." [1]

Marketing is an act that brings attention to and connects a consumer with a desired product. The products on the shelves and tables at this festival booth were there long before Josh and his father had arrived. Potential consumers strolled by and paid only a modicum of attention. Then something highlighted the products in a new light. Drama, humor, action, words were useful in drawing in customers.

You have a message, a voice, and a desire to broadcast it out. You know to whom you want to broadcast to, your ideal audience. Somewhere out there the perfect recipient is juggling questions and concerns in their minds that your voice can truly address. They need you; you need them. Marketing is the act that will help you find each other.

Discovering ways to get the attention of your ideal audience, then letting them in on who you are and what you can do for them is at the heart of marketing and promotions. This includes having a solid brand, or identity. When that identity is in perfect focus it is easy to present that picture in the form of marketing.

BRANDING

On a trip to Houston, Texas one early summer, I was taken to the George Ranch Historical Park. Established in 1824 this 23,000-acre ranch follows a family history from when Texas was still a part of Mexico through current times. Today, many generations later, the Fort Bend landmark is still a working ranch.

I was perched on wooden bleachers at a small dusty arena. It sported cowboys demonstrating their skill in roping and medicating livestock. The riders worked in unity with the beautiful horses beneath them. Each of the animals had branding seared into their hide.

It was explained that by the markings you could determine from a distance who the owner of the animal was, the identity of the animal was, their sire, dame, and date of birth. While roaming the grounds on a frosty morning a cowboy can detect any animal based on the branding.

As an animal needs the proper branding. So does every product and effort on the market. It is never beneficial to use false advertising or to promote yourself as something you are not. There can be a draw in padding your resume, but your ideal audience will remain faithful when you entice them with truth and engage them by authentic means. Marketing and promotion done right requires a needed product, trusted permanence, and effective promotion.

The most powerful branding leaves an indelible impression. The most effective impressions create an emotional connection. An emotional connection creates loyalty and loyalty grows your brand.

Nike, the multinational corporation most known for making footwear and sports attire, has a very recognizable brand and emotive connection. The name is derived from the winged Greek deity, Nike, who personified victory. The trademark swoosh is an arc that represents motion and speed. Nike has utilized the promotional phrase, "Just do it." It is found on commercials, apparel, and wristbands alike. There is an emotive motivation and association with confidence, leadership, and triumph. All of this said in a name, an emblem, and a phrase.

So, before buying billboard space, designing your marquee, or promoting yourself on social media, get your product branded and ready for marketing. It can take months before you have everything running smoothly. In the process, stay true to your identity and branding.

Who are you, what do you stand for, and how does your audience fit in to it all? Music, logos, pictures, message, what you wear, your speech, lesson shared, and every other aspect of your effort should be sifted through the filter of your branding identity.

10 SECOND COMMERCIAL

The ten-second commercial is a marketing tool that puts your message in a concise form that you can easily share. It is meant to encapsulate who you are and what you can do for your audience in one or two sentences. It can also be referred to as an elevator speech. If you met someone in an elevator who asked you about your efforts, what would you say in the time before the doors open and you are both on your way?

Before you move into the realm of marketing, know what you're about and what you have to offer. Make it so concise that you can explain it in ten-seconds time.

TYPES OF MARKETING

There seems to be as many ways to get the word out as there are stars in the heavens. When choosing which star system you are aiming for remember who you are (your brand) and who your ideal audience is. Your marketing and promotions will be a reflection of that relationship. You are not likely to be successful if you are marketing your brand of condoms in a convent. It is not your target market.

When choosing from the wide range of possibilities, follow these guidelines:

1 Remember who you are (your brand).

2 Remember who your target audience is, what they are doing, what

they pay attention to, what they are reading, watching, and listening to.

3 Be mindful of what others, like you or your 'competition,' may be doing.

4 Have your 10 second commercial, logos, and other branding aids at the ready.

5 Filter everything through your branding.

PHONE A FRIEND

Your friends and family already love you and should naturally want your efforts to succeed. Ask them to listen and comment. If you have acquaintances that are not supportive do not include them. Criticism is fabulous. Skepticism can grant good advice and help you improve. Lack of support and extreme negativity will steal your energy. This type of marketing is word of mouth marketing. Your loyal audience likes you and your product. Ask them to invite others who would benefit from your efforts.

A commercial that was an example of viral marketing hit this point home in the 1980's. It implored users to spread the word. If you tell two friends about Faberge Organics Shampoo with wheat germ oil and honey, "then they'll tell two friends, and they'll tell two friends, and so on, and so on, and so on." [2] This tell two friends ad was a market-ing success. You can have success when utilizing this simple method of marketing.

ASK FOR REVIEWS

Reviews can create excitement. People like to like what other people like. Ask someone either known to your audience or just known to you to write a review. Post it on your web page, description, or social media site. Let others know that people like them find value in your work.

EMAIL

Emails can be an intimate and inexpensive way to share your efforts. Email marketing is arguably the most effective way to connect. There is a balance between sharing your message and sending annoying junk mail. Make a short, attractive, relevant piece. Avoid text heavy emails, which often get quickly discarded. Most experts recommend a frequency of at least every 30 days.

Be mindful of privacy. When sending out your messages to multiple recipients, use the BCC field in your message's address. This makes the email addresses of others invisible to others. It protects privacy. BCC stands for blind carbon copy.

There are services that will email blast for you, you can also create messages yourself. Publishing software and newsletter creators will easily create messages to share your brand and highlight your efforts. Many of these have ready-to-use templates that you simply fill in with your own information.

Keep your email organized. It can be much like the outline of your broadcast with a hook, story, lesson, ask. Include pictures, relevant links, and if possible, other media.

The point is to build support. For those who want to connect, make sure you make it easy for them. Have your branding, logo, and contact information visible. For those who do not want to connect, you do not want to go where you are not wanted. Make sure that people can unsubscribe or opt out.

BE OUR GUEST

If you can get featured on another show, you have instantly opened yourself up to a whole new group of potential audience members. Conversely, having guests on that will promote you or let their audience know that they will be on your show, allows someone else to do some of the marketing work for you.

After an interview, send your guest a link to the show and embedded codes of the interview, if this is within your wheelhouse. Embedded codes allow for someone to insert a music player or video of your project directly into a website. Making it easy for a guest to post their interview will give them a way to highlight their voice and give yours a ready promotion.

SOCIAL MEDIA

We would need a separate book if we were to cover all the aspects of this astounding social networking tool. It has been said that networking is at the heart of marketing. If true, then social media would be a networking promotional tool on steroids.

Social media is free and accessible to most everybody. According to Statista, "In 2020, over 223 million Americans were using social networks to post pictures, like and comment on content by others, or send private messages. With over 70 percent of the U.S. population holding a social media account, these platforms and services have become some of the most popular online activities of the past couple decades. By 2025, the number of social network users in the United States is forecast to increase to approximately 243 million." [3] You have access to all of this for free.

Here are some ways to use social media for effective marketing:

Announcing your broadcast
Let people know when it will be, what it will be about, and how people can listen. Place your hook front and center and see if you can catch an audience.

Post in groups
It is more important to show that you are part of a group than simply post ads for your broadcast or project. Establish yourself in large groups on social media. Like, comment, and post. These are like-minded people. When it is time to share your broadcast, they will already know and appreciate you.

Ask questions
Ask your network what they might want to hear about. This will benefit you in two important ways. First, you can garner great ideas for upcoming episodes. Second, you build interest.

Place ads
For just a few dollars you can put your post or page before thousands of individuals that marketing algorithms indicate are most interested in you and your broadcast.

Video shorts
Video shorts are seen on Facebook, YouTube, TikTok, Instagram,

Twitter, and dozens of other sites. You might take audio and create pictures in a short video of under four minutes. Another popular format is posting yourself giving commentary. Shorts are powerful and can build your audience quickly. When making a short be sure that you use it as a funnel to drive people to your site or broadcast.

Create interest

Create interest by offering something. At a county fair, surrounded by the smell of cotton candy and the rows of booths, salesmen hawk wares. They may offer a cool trinket or a chance to win a trip for two to a fishing expedition in Alaska. They do this to attract potential consumers and increase sales. For you, creating a buzz can generate interest. You can do this by offering a gift, a free download, a prize, or any other engagement gimmick. Offer a book, a free download, or elicit comments.

Post like a madman

If you are a company that makes breakfast cereal, your chances of selling boxes will greatly increase if those boxes are on as many shelves, in as many stores as possible. Putting your projects on multiple channels, outlets, and platforms does the same for your broadcast. If it is a blog, a book, a video, a lecture, post it like a madman.

Clickbait

Clickbait is a kind of hook. Using a picture, subject line, or some other means to entice someone to click through and then be funneled to another site. Clickbait is a teaser that draws people in. You can use short quotes, a small video from your production, a post or comment on social media. Whatever it may be, an effective hook and an ask to "click here for more", can funnel someone to your broadcast, website, or page.

HASHTAGS & SEOs

Like the words on a street sign, SEOs and hashtags direct traffic to your location. SEO is an acronym for Search Engine Optimization. They are words that are associated with your page or post that search engines use to direct people to content that they are searching for.

Likewise, hashtags, developed as a way to organize topics and conversations on social media platforms, act much the same way. As you post your projects, most platforms allow you to utilize hashtags. Your title, description, and hashtags go out into the ethos, floating about until someone's search connects them to it.

Careful attention to these world wide web street signs is a great way to get the word out. They direct traffic to your location. Additionally, SEO is an established and foundational element to anyone and anything relying on online searches.

PAY-PER-CLICK

Pay-per-click advertising is where you bid on keywords and pay for clicks that appear at the top of search engine result pages or SERPs. This approach targets potential customers who are actively searching for something that you offer.

SPONSORSHIP

Whatever your niche there is a person or an organization that aligns with your vision. They may be the perfect match for sponsorship. A sponsorship of monetary value can offset the monthly cost of your production.

There is also sponsorship though promotion. An organization might give you space on their own webpage or newsletters. This, in turn, will funnel people to you.

Another type of sponsorship is affiliate marketing. This is where you make an agreement with a company to talk about their products, post them on your pages, and encourage your audience to make a purchase. The company will give you a special link and a discount for those who use it. In return you can make a percentage from a sale that comes from that link. Some companies will have a list of affiliates or influencers and recommend their sites.

CHOOSE WISELY

There are two basic approaches to promoting. There is single focus marketing or multiple focus. A single focus puts all of your eggs into one basket, all of your resources and energy into one marketing outlet. A multi-focus method diversifies your efforts. If you are going it alone or have a very specific audience, a single focus may work. Multi-focused approaches can get your message before more eyes but can drain you of time and energy. Whatever you do, choose wisely. One of the biggest killers of passion is burn out.

When your product is well in place, brand it. Be consistent with it. That permanence will establish you in your market. When your product and permanence is well set, research the ways you might promote your efforts.

Like the 12-year-old boy, Josh, at a Highland Games booth. He brought down the house with his out of the box thinking and humor. The best way to market is to employ the unique things that make you, YOU. Seek out ways to reach that very special person, your ideal audience. Just try not to do it without the use of a very sharp knife in your hand.

There is a myriad of marketing options out there. There is only one option that will elevate you better than any other. It is the real authentic you. You are your best billboard.

[1] American Marketing Association. 2017. What is Marketing? — The Definition of Marketing — AMA. [online] Available at: <https://www.ama.org/the-definition-of-marketing-what-is-marketing/> [Accessed 16 October 2021].

[2] Youtube.com. 1986. [online] Available at: <https://www.youtube.com/watch?v=-EtRss-gIac> [Accessed 18 October 2021].

[3] Statista. 2021. Topic: Social media usage in the United States . [online] Available at: <https://www.statista.com/topics/3196/social-media-usage-in-the-united-states/#dossierKeyfigures> [Accessed 18 October 2021].

22

PITCH YOUR PROJECT

Pitching is inevitable. Pitching is something every person must do at some point in their life. You pitch yourself when applying for a job, getting into college, or when you propose marriage to the one you love. You pitch products when looking for sales.

The pitch building process is used in every area of communications. Landing pages on the web benefit from this focused message. Podcasters need it for creating intros, outs, and summaries for grabbing their audience's attention. Authors use it to get published, produce book summaries, and to send out queries for interviews. Pitching to a customer, publicist, producer, or investor is an absolute must if you have a business idea, podcast, book, or project. In the business and communications world, one of the best ways to share your passion is by writing and presenting a successful pitch.

A pitch is a brief message selling yourself, your project, or idea. It is a presentation of your concept in a condensed message for film, television, print media, investments, or any other purpose that benefits your project. Your pitch is used to raise funds, gather support, or secure a commitment for production. A good pitch can turn your idea into a viable and profitable venture.

First impressions count. We dive into this idea in previous books, our master class, and podcast. Fine-tune your message to produce the 10, 30, or 60 second personal commercial. It's also called an elevator speech, which is an intro to your project given in the time it would take to share with a stranger on an elevator ride. Your ideas condensed into a dynamic summary can be built upon for longer presentations like a five-to-twenty-minute in person pitch, interviews, and the one page that can be used in email correspondence, as a promotion piece, or referenced in your interviews.

Think of yourself as a baker. Now imagine a fresh from the oven plate of delicious cookies. The way they look is so tempting and their alluring smell entices. Pass those by potential customers and you've got their attention. They will want to know more about your menu of baked goods just from that one interaction with a cookie. One taste and they're ready to indulge in more. The cookies are like your pitch, they are a fantastic representation of what it is that you have to offer.

Today I will give you the recipe for a great pitch. A recipe can take your kitchen full of ingredients and transform the bag of flour, carton of eggs, package of chocolate chips, and the stick of butter from raw elements into something that sells. Our lesson today will take the elements of your message and mix them into a powerful presentation.

The following are the ingredients of any pitch and how they utilize the the hook, story, lesson, ask concept and communication superpowers of engagement, entertainment, information, and inspiration. Remember that if you are lacking in any of these powers, shore them up. Call on your super friends and colleagues, if necessary. This ensures the most powerful and dynamic pitch.

FIRST INGREDIENT
THE TAGLINE: HOOK / ENGAGEMENT
A tagline is a short phrase that describes your brand. The tagline of any project is the lesson, the purpose, and promise you make to your target audience. The tagline is a slogan that grabs attention and creates an engaging connection with your audience.

Great taglines create a need for your project and keep your brand at the forefront of your audience's mind. Think Wheaties' "breakfast of champions," Nike's "just do it," Taco Bell's "think outside the bun," or Skittles' "taste the rainbow". Encapsulate your main message into a catchy phrase that connects, and you will have a winning tag line.

Create your tagline with these three elements, brand , benefits, and some brilliance. The brand part is the focus of what you do. The benefit is why you are needed or how you meet a need. The brilliance is your promise to your audience or customer. While you want to be catchy it is better to be clear than clever or silly.

TAGLINE FOR PODCAST

Legacy Laughter Example: "The more you laugh the "father" you go" The brand, Legacy Laughter, is represented by "laugh". The benefit part is "the father (or farther) you go". The brilliance is the promise that is implied, if you laugh with us the farther you will get in life as a father.

STORY TAGLINES

The Wizard of Oz example: "You don't have to go over the rainbow to see that there is no place like home"

"The book 80 million read! The play 941 cities saw! Now the greatest Technicolor movie ever made will take you over the rainbow."

SECOND INGREDIENT
THE LOGLINE: LESSON / INFORMATION

Scrolling through endless movie posters on streaming services, you stop on something that catches your eye. Before you watch the trailer, you read a short snippet about the film. This synopsis is the logline. It employs the information superpower in your pitch by educating your audience with a one sentence straight forward look at what your project is about.

A logline is usually between about ten and sixty words. It is your project, book, podcast, seminar, or message in a nutshell. It highlights your subject, the challenge or goal, and the solution or method.

For a novel, movie, or television pitch, the logline follows this simple recipe of protagonist , goal , antagonist . These three elements presented properly encapsulate your story or message. Your logline helps us understand who or what this subject or antagonist is. The goal is what the subject must accomplish. The antagonist is the struggle, challenge or challenger faced to achieve the goal.

LOGLINE FOR PODCASTS and COMMUNICATION PROJECTS

There is no end to the competition for your audience's time so you must grab their attention right off the bat. A logline for podcasts is a brief description of what you offer.

EXAMPLES FOR PODCASTS

The Ramsey Show example : Take control of your ("your" = you are the protagonist) life and money once and for all. The Ramsey Show offers straight talk from Dave Ramsey and his team of co-hosts. Millions listen as callers from all walks of life learn how to get out of debt (debt is the protagonist) and start building for the future (goal).

Legacy Laughter example: Fathers (protagonist) have it tough these days, so (antagonist) grab a beer and a few laughs with Joe Giggle and his comedian friends, then walk away with insight, support, and hope (goal).

LOGLINE EXAMPLES FOR STORIES, FILM, TV, BOOKS

Star Wars example : A farm boy (protagonist) from a desert planet teams up with a feisty princess, a mercenary space pilot and an old wizard to form a ragtag rebellion (goal) against the evil Galactic Empire (antagonist).

Casablanca example : A cynical expatriate café owner (protagonist) must decide if he will help his former love and her fugitive husband escape (goal) the Nazis in French Morocco (antagonist).

The Wizard of Oz example: A tornado sweeps a young girl (protagonist) away to a magical land where she must overcome an evil witch and strange challenges (antagonist) to find her way home (goal).

THIRD INGREDIENT
THE SYNOPSIS: STORY / ENTERTAINMENT

The synopsis is the entertaining portion of your pitch. It puts the cinematic wow of your project into succinct words. Think of your synopsis as a short verbal trailer for your pitch. This trailer should employ the superpower of entertainment, pulling out every sparkling, exciting, entertaining element you can to dazzle the imagination.

There is something called the hero's Journey. Professor of literature and author, Joseph Campbell, found that all compelling tales have a universal pattern. It is what he referred to as the monomyth. In his book, The Hero with a Thousand Faces , he showed how all stories have different characters, settings, and cultures. They may come from diverse eras and geographical locations, but from Shakespeare to George Lucas, the "hero's journey" is the same.

Here is how it works. Beyond the "beginning, middle, and end" of a story, there is the following pattern. It starts with the journey of a protagonist or "hero". Something happens and the hero must answer the call or deal with a problem. They go into action and face a main obstacle we call the antagonist . They complete the challenge and return changed, which is the goal . This can also be referred to as part of the character arc.

The synopsis brings the characters, the setting, the challenges, or conflicts to life. It introduces the hero and their main companions from the hero's journey. The more compelling and familiar your characters become in your synopsis, the more successful your pitch will be. Do this by using extraordinary adjectives and descriptive words that accurately portray the characters and their mission.

Here are the elements of the synopsis.

1 The main character(s) or protagonist(s) – with defining characteristics and motives.

2 The goal

3 The stakes – why is the goal vital

4 The antagonist or challenge to the goal

5 The plot points or key events

6 The conclusion

Here are some basic rules for creating a synopsis. A synopsis is usually one to five pages, limited on average to about 500 words, and takes less than five minutes to read. For podcasts the synopsis is much shorter. Whatever your project, make it concise. Use all caps for the first usage of your characters. Keep the tone in the appropriate genre. For example, if it is a comedy, use light-hearted verbiage. Communicate in the third person. Write in the present tense. Introduce characters with accurate, memorable, and vibrant descriptions. Explain their motives and responses to their challenges.

Writing a synopsis is a good skill to develop. A proven way to grow your skill in synopsis creation is to narrate movie trailers. Write what you see colorfully, accurately, and concisely.

SYNOPSIS FOR THE PODCAST

Legacy Laughter: Funny man JOE GIGGLY is a husband, father, factory worker, and avid micro beer drinker, when he has time to indulge. Sneaking out to his man cave in the garage he turns on his mike and light beer sign then invites fellow comedians, interesting guests, callers, and friends to grab a cold one and connect. He uses humor and anecdotes to leave fathers in these tough times with insight, support, and hope.

SYNOPSIS FOR THE FILM

The Wizard of Oz example: DOROTHY GALE, a Kansas farm girl has her dog taken for destruction by ALMIRA GULCH, a bitter neighbor. She whisks him away on her bicycle, but Toto escapes. Dorothy, longing for a different life "Over the Rainbow", runs away with Toto. They come to the wagon of the kindly professor and fortune-teller who tricks Dorothy into believing that her aunt has had a heart attack because she ran away. Dorothy rushes home while a cyclone approaches. Dorothy is hit on the head by a window and knocked unconscious. She revives to find the house inside the cyclone and Miss Gulch on her bicycle turning into a witch on a broomstick. The house comes to rest in the colorful Land of Oz. It lands on the Wicked Witch of the East, killing her. GLINDA, the Good Witch of the North removes the witch's magical ruby slippers, giving them to Dorothy. The WICKED WITCH OF THE WEST arrives for slippers, but to no avail. The Witch vows revenge. Dorothy asks how to get home and Glinda suggests that Dorothy follow the yellow brick road to the Emerald City, for the Wizard of Oz's help. Along the way, Dorothy meets a SCARECROW, who longs for a brain, TIN MAN, who wants a heart, and a COWARDLY LION who desires courage. Dorothy suggests that they all go to seek the Wizard's help. They face dangers and attacks but finally reach the Emerald City. There the Wizard appears as a terrifying apparition. He agrees to grant their requests if they bring him the broomstick of the Wicked Witch. On their way to the witch's castle, the witch's army of winged monkeys capture Dorothy and Toto. Dorothy offers her ruby slippers, but they will not come off if Dorothy is alive. As the witch decides how to kill Dorothy, Toto escapes, finds Dorothy's friends, and leads them to the castle. The witch's guards surround them, and the witch sets fire to Scarecrow. Dorothy tosses a bucket of water at him splashing the witch, who then melts. They bring the broomstick to the Wizard who resists keeping his promise. Toto finds him behind a curtain revealing that he is just a man. He rewards the friends and confesses that he is a balloonist from Kansas. He offers to take Dorothy home in his balloon. As they prepare to leave, Toto is taunted by a cat and leaps from the balloon, Dorothy goes after him and the balloon takes off. Dorothy is broken-hearted but Glinda tells Dorothy that she has always had the power to return home. Dorothy bids her friends goodbye and follow's Glinda's instructions to click her heels three times and to think to herself, "There's no place like home." She awakens to find her loved ones around her. Dorothy says she loves them all and that she will never leave again because, "There is no place like home."

EXTRA INGREDIENTS
INCLUDING THE ASK / INSPIRATION

You can take a basic cookie recipe and add to it nuts, sprinkles, or frosting. Likewise, add elements to your pitch as appropriate for the circumstances. You might add a character layout, listing your main characters then highlighting their attributes. Steer clear of detailing secondary characters. Mes-en-scene can be added which is your vision of the scene design, set, and arrangement of actors in scenes for storyboarding a theatre or film production. You might add the time period of your story, budget, and demographic info.

Your pitch, in its completion, is essentially an ask. You are seeking support, investment, or action. Many forget to add that all important action call or objective to their pitch. What would you like your pitch to accomplish, what are you asking for? Give the right recipient the opportunity to participate by providing a clear mission.

Whatever your project, completing a pitch on one sheet of paper, known as a "one page", compiles your passion into a succinct vision. Do your best to keep this document down to one side of one sheet of paper. You will find this one sheet pitch invaluable to your focus, branding, and promotion as you move forward in sharing your voice.

23

DON'T STOP BELIEVING

Rugby is an English-founded full-contact sport that might be described as a hybrid of soccer and American football, albeit without pads or helmets. Rugby is popular all over the world, but it wasn't until 2018 that MLR, Major League Rugby, came to the United States. The Seattle Seawolves were one of 13 professional Major League Rugby teams in the U.S. at that time. My experience with covering the team is a reminder of why the heart of what you do is by far more important than the tools, the planning, and the process.

Sports is a piece of my on-air repertoire so you can imagine the thrill of covering my hometown's MLR Team in its inaugural year! It was a goose bump moment at the Seattle Seawolves' 4,000-capacity stadium when I found myself an unwritten part of local sports history.

Unlike many other sports where you will find the coach barking orders from the sideline, in Rugby matches the coach can sit in a media box above the pitch. As a member of the media, in that same box, I was seated next to the head coach during the very first home game.

The team was still finding their footing in broadcasting, in set up, and in making team/fan traditions. Before this match, they had not gotten a plan in place to have someone lead the national anthem. So, the announcer asked that everyone simply observe the flag. Then the audience, like the Canadian fans from Edmonton that I previously mentioned, began to sing the national anthem together. It was disjointed and off tune but one of the most beautiful sounds I had ever experienced.

I sang along, the sole voice in the media booth. I am always one to sing and even shed a tear during the anthem. Afterwards the coach turned to me and said, "That was amazing. We need to have you back to sing the anthem." Humbled, I thanked him but said that the beauty of people sincerely singing our nation's anthem was more moving than any singer could portray. The rest of the games throughout the year you would hear the announcer say, "As is our tradition we will have the audience sing the national anthem."

I smiled every time I heard that announcement. It drives home a vital point. A well-produced message is important, but an important message need not be well produced to make a difference. Please do not let the need for perfection and ultimate professionalism hinder you from speaking your voice.

I remember a story from my youth that illustrates how the under anticipated can have unexpected results. I was seven. My parents had phoned the police, volunteers drove around anxiously searching, and the mothers of myself and my fellow seven-year-old friend stood by the phone desperate for word of our whereabouts. Haggy and I were participating in a charity walk-a-thon where participants get pledges for each mile of the twenty-mile course that they made. It had been hours since we were last seen.

That morning my mother made sure we dressed in comfortable shoes with backpacks full of snacks, drinks, extra socks, foot powder, and a fully equipped first air kit that could have provided triage for a small army. Perhaps it was overkill, especially considering that no one anticipated we two young girls would walk more than a mile, maybe, just maybe, two. We started out in the morning and by early evening no one had heard from us.

The sun threatened to set on this fund-raising event, as the last of the walkers were making their way to the finish line. Finally, in the distance, one of our fathers caught sight of two little girls with their big backpacks waddling wearily towards them. Twenty miles, nearly ten hours later, we had finished the course.

It seemed unbelievable, no one anticipated our resolve. Our parents' first thought was of relief that we were safe, the second was of shock and concern that family members had pledged between twenty and two hundred dollars per mile, thinking we would only make it a short distance.

There is something to be said for pure resolve. Having good equipment is a blessing, focusing your niche for a specific audience will grow your efforts, having a well laid foundation and a proper platform will grant clarity. These are important aspects. But never allow your lack of equipment or experience to keep you from getting that important message to the waiting world!

Even those who have been around the communications block a few times run into unexpected challenges. Professionals find themselves in unfamiliar territory. People in the know can realize there are things that they just do not know.

Wherever you are on your communications journey, never underestimate yourself! You have been imparted with a passion for a purpose. You are reading this book for a reason. Its message will have a role in your life. So, whatever you do, keep going, do not lose heart, and never, ever stop believing in your voice!

You have a passion and purpose. My passion is to empower your voice so that you can change the world!

You can find more help and power up your voice at www.findyourvoice.fun. There, we can help you start your broadcast, publish your book, publicize you, and help you FIND YOUR VOICE!

Thank you for allowing me to be part of your journey!

Michelle

Michelle Mendoza is a dynamic broadcasting professional. She has been on radio, television, stage, and screen from her home town in Seattle, WA, throughout the U.S. and U.K.. She has created multi-platform, multi-medium programs for herself and many others. As a motivational & public speaker, actress, cultural dancer, singer-songwriter, Michelle has both the experience and training that makes communications second nature to her. Michelle lives a joy-filled life surrounded by friends and family in the Pacific Northwest.

www.ingramcontent.com/pod-product-compliance
Lightning Source LLC
Chambersburg PA
CBHW060542130626
46553CB00002B/870